TIPS AND OTHER BRIGHT IDEAS FOR SECONDARY SCHOOL LIBRARIES

TIPS
AND OTHER BRIGHT IDEAS

for Secondary School Libraries

Volume 4
Kate Vande Brake, Editor

LINWORTH

AN IMPRINT OF ABC-CLIO, LLC
Santa Barbara, California • Denver, Colorado • Oxford, England

Copyright 2010 by ABC-CLIO, LLC

All rights reserved. No part of this publication may be reproduced, stored in a retrieval system, or transmitted, in any form or by any means, electronic, mechanical, photocopying, recording, or otherwise, except for the inclusion of brief quotations in a review, without prior permission in writing from the publisher.

Library of Congress Cataloging-in-Publication Data

Tips and other bright ideas for secondary school libraries.
   Volume 4 / Kate Vande Brake, editor.
     p. cm.
   ISBN 978-1-58683-418-0 (acid-free paper) — ISBN 978-1-58683-419-7 (ebook)   1. High school libraries—United States—Administration.
I. Vande Brake, Kate.
   Z675.S3T4945   2010
   025.1'978223—dc22   2010010428

ISBN: 978-1-58683-418-0
EISBN: 978-1-58683-419-7

14 13 12 11 10   1 2 3 4 5

This book is also available on the World Wide Web as an eBook.
Visit www.abc-clio.com for details.

Linworth
An Imprint of ABC-CLIO, LLC

ABC-CLIO, LLC
130 Cremona Drive, P.O. Box 1911
Santa Barbara, California 93116-1911

This book is printed on acid-free paper ∞

Manufactured in the United States of America

TABLE OF CONTENTS

Introduction..................................vii

Section 1: Managing the Library..........................1
- Administration...................................3
- Arrangement.....................................7
- Furniture..9
- Signage, Displays, and Bulletin Boards................10
- Appearance and Order............................17
- Supplies..22
- Equipment......................................24
- Acquisitions....................................31
- Processing Books and Materials....................33

Section 2: Working with Students in the Library..........36
- Students.......................................38
- Overdue Books..................................43

Section 3: Teaching Research Skills....................45
- Library Orientation..............................47
- Before a Research Project........................51
- During a Research Project........................52
- After a Research Project.........................54

Section 4: Collaborating with Teachers.................55
- Attracting Teachers to the Library.................57
- Promoting Library Materials......................60
- Working Together................................62
- Integrating Curricula.............................65

Section 5: Using Technology in the Library 67
        Computers 69
        Printing 71
        Web Sites 72
        E-mail 74
        Searching the Internet 76
        Useful Library Applications 77

Section 6: Promoting Reading 80
        Book Talks, Displays, and Bulletin Boards 82
        Reading Incentives 89
        Student Recommendations 92
        Special Events 96
        Special Tactics 101
        Utilizing Technology 107

Section 7: Building Positive Public Relations 109
        Teachers and Staff 111
        Students 115
        Parents and Community 118
        Special Events 122

Section 8: Working with Helpers 124
        Students 126
        Volunteers 128

About the Editor 130

INTRODUCTION

One decade into the 21st century, school libraries across the United States are leaders in technology innovation. Today's libraries are riding the tail of the Internet and the World Wide Web to blaze an amazing path of technology and information assets for adolescent patrons. From Wikis to Nings to library Web pages chock-full of resources and interactive tools, libraries have come a very long way in a very short time.

Librarians are leaders in the field of information literacy and information technology. They teach their patrons to embrace new technologies. Today's librarians are media specialists—experts in books and media, inquiry and research, and information technology. Although most adults can learn new technologies on an as-needed basis, library media specialists stay about 10 steps ahead, ready for each new query and armed with possible leads to find answers.

Library media specialists' jobs are complicated by today's economic situation. Our attitudes about how we spend our time and our budgets are highly influenced by the continuing budget decreases and rumors that circulate regarding which positions will be cut each spring as our districts contemplate programs to sacrifice.

In the early 1990s, the first volume of *Tips and Other Bright Ideas for School Librarians* was published. Subsequent editions offered more great money- and time-saving tips for school librarians. A new edition is now born as library media specialists have continued to offer their advice, practical knowledge, and experience to a vast network of lifelong learners eager to improve their media programs and continue to positively impact their school communities.

Because secondary school librarians are responsible for the management of their media centers and the volunteers and staff who help with the daily operations, it is up to them to promote their media center materials through programs, special events, and creative activities. The responsibility of teaching students research and citation skills as well as other information literacy skills has become more and more crucial as students continue in their education and become contributing members of society in the 21st century.

Creating an inclusive, inviting, and learning-conducive environment is another powerful responsibility that school librarians assume with vigor. Whether the librarian is designing displays promoting new books or mounting bulletins boards highlighting authors, students, or teachers, she knows that the physical facility impacts learning and that marketing the media center is critical. Simple procedures such as keeping extra supplies and equipment for teachers and students demonstrate that the library is the place to find the answers to life's questions as well as an MP3 player and a headset.

Collaboration with other teachers is vital in today's educational setting. Technology is a key component of successful collaboration between the librarian, the collaborating teacher, and the collaborative project. Technology is used to stretch students' imaginations, strengthen their engagement, and increase their understanding and achievement.

In this same vein, the librarian is also the technology expert in the building—the go-to person when the DVD player isn't working or when the projector is not projecting. From storing manuals for the technical equipment in the school to managing the checkout system for the various remote controls and cables to serving as copyright guru, the school librarian is on the job and making a difference.

Librarians balance meager budgets, implement their collection development plans, arrange the library's vast media catalogs, and develop processes for their collections. They are often responsible for their own budgets and must balance the need for new books with the need to replace old books. Some librarians are fortunate enough to have books processed for them, but many times the librarian must find the time to process her own acquisitions. Often she must dust her books, fix book bindings, tape ripped pages, and dry the occasional wet page.

The librarian of today is at the center of his school. He develops his collection, discovering new materials for students and teachers in the building; she builds the bridges between grade levels and subjects and challenges and encourages the students. She sees the big picture and serves as the heart of the school, pumping energy and information to all.

The tips included in this edition of *Tips and Other Bright Ideas for Secondary School Libraries* showcase the ingenuity and creativity of today's librarian.

The tips in this book are organized into the following nine sections:

- Managing the Library
- Working with Students in the Library
- Teaching Research Skills
- Collaborating with Teachers
- Using Technology in the Library
- Promoting Reading
- Building Positive Public Relations
- Working with Helpers

Please use the creative and practical tips included in this volume to help provide you with some fresh and invigorating ideas that may solve some of your ongoing challenges or simply make your job easier.

Some of these tips may sound familiar because you are already implementing similar ideas in your own media center. When you have other great ideas, please submit them to Library Media Connection. You can contact LMC online at http://www.linworth.com/lmc. Thanks for sharing your expertise through collaboration to strengthen library media programs across this country for students, teachers, and colleagues.

SECTION 1:

MANAGING THE LIBRARY

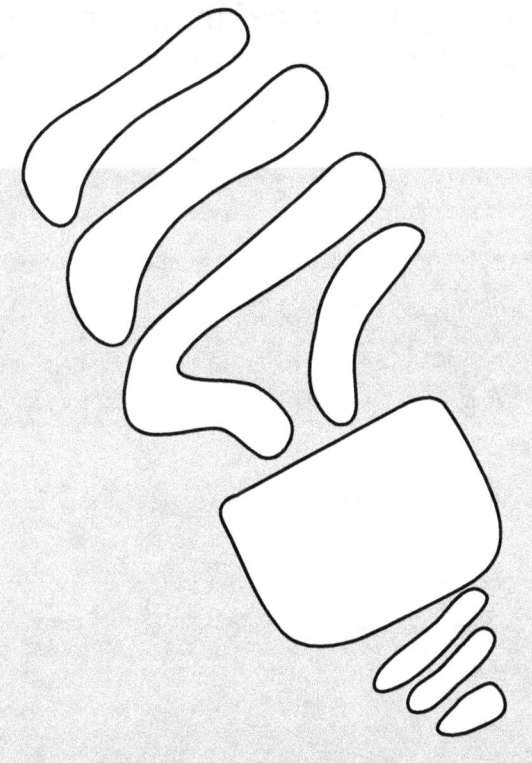

School libraries have many functions. They are a classroom; they are a research facility. They can hold special events or be a quiet retreat. The librarian and her staff must wear many hats to fulfill the needs of every patron, from rearranging chairs and displays to recommending new books to eager readers to teaching information literacy skills.

Deciding how to arrange the furniture, display books, and organize the checkout process is one of the roles of the librarian that has a positive impact on students and staff. A library media center that operates smoothly creates a welcoming and inclusive climate in the school.

The tips included in this section have been divided into the following topics:

- Administration
- Arrangement
- Furniture
- Signage, Displays, and Bulletin Boards
- Appearance and Order
- Supplies
- Equipment
- Acquisitions
- Processing Books and Materials

ADMINISTRATION

Business Cards

Business cards are our professional interface with the world. Every librarian needs business cards, even if they are homemade. Office supply stores carry blank decorative business cards that can be run through a home printer. A Google Images search will yield plenty of library-themed art to be printed on simple card stock.

Sheryl Kindle Fullner, Nooksack Valley Middle School, Everson, Washington • April/May 2007

Media Bee

Instead of a Quilting Bee, schedule a Media Bee as part of monthly district library meetings. The Bee rotates through all the libraries. Each building librarian in turn selects a job that could be tackled in a 30- to 45-minute time slot and prepares an appropriate number of staplers, scissors, computers, and so on, so that peer librarians can make a big dent in those jobs that are too daunting to tackle alone—for example, the nefarious *back room*.

Sheryl Kindle Fullner, Nooksack Valley Middle School, Everson, Washington • October 2008

Post-a-Note

There are several inexpensive Web-based companies from which to buy postcards. Design your own media center postcards and use them to send friendly notes to staff, parents, and others. Put your favorite reading quote along with your name, the name of your school, and your e-mail address or phone number. Keep them by your computer, and you will use them often!

Catherine Trinkle, Hickory Elementary,
Avon, Indiana • August/September 2008

Thank-You Supplies

Stock your desk drawer with a box of thank-you cards, a box of sympathy cards, a box of blank note cards with a multipurpose design (e.g., flowers, mountain scenes, etc.), and a book of "forever" stamps. You will then have these materials handy for sending thank-you notes to colleagues, administrators, sales reps, and others who go out of their way to support your library program. It will also facilitate sending sympathy cards and other greetings to coworkers.

Amy Pickett, Ridley High School,
Folsom, Pennsylvania • August/September 2008

Be Prepared

At the beginning of the school year, type out a checklist for library substitutes and laminate it, with one copy for the office and one copy for your library. In addition to the various user names and passwords, describe where light switches, thermostats, computer switches, and copier switches are located. Spell out storm procedures such as unplugging cords or how to use surge protectors (and where they are located). Describe where the emergency procedure folder is located in the event of fires, terrorist attacks, floods, blizzards, earthquakes, and so on. Include a few jobs that always need to be done.

Sheryl Kindle Fullner, Nooksack Valley Middle School,
Everson, Washington • January/February 2009

Logging In

To simplify instructions for a substitute, do a screen capture (usually Shift+Print Screen) of each step of the log-on process. Then paste and print these visuals in sequence in your sub folder. There is nothing like coming back from a bad illness or accident to find that a sub has not been able to log on, and the library is littered with sticky notes of students' first names and vague book titles. In our district, log-on IDs change regularly, so the folder needs to be updated every time the password changes.

Sheryl Kindle Fullner, Nooksack Valley Middle School,
Everson, Washington • May/June 2009

Measuring Up

Library workers often need to measure things. Instead of reaching for a ruler or tape measure, attach a measuring gauge to the outside top edge your keyboard drawer for instant availability. Rulers and tapes that are as thin as a piece of cardboard are easy to find, or just photocopy any flat tape measure onto an overhead transparency and trim to fit your space. Hold securely with wide library tape wrapping around the edge of the drawer.

Sheryl Kindle Fullner, Nooksack Valley Middle School,
Everson, Washington • May/June 2009

Drill and Practice

Keep informational tidbits you want to remember on a daily calendar such as Microsoft Outlook. Enter the item so that it repeats itself for a few weeks or even months. Each morning, the hint or new term is visible, so that you can learn new terms or ideas quickly. It's great for copyright ideas from Carol Simpson, for information from Joe Huber of LMC, for terms such as OSS (open source software), or even for new Web sites.

Donna Walters, Valparaiso (Indiana) High School • May/June 2009

Tracking the Notes

Taking a few minutes to note personal successes, dissatisfactions, and potential ideas for the future—as well as soliciting comments and suggestions from others at the conclusion of library media program events—is most helpful. Place the notes along with the CD-ROM that stores documents related to the event (flyers, emails, letters, etc.) in a binder for easy retrieval.

Vanessa Fortenberry, Stoneview Elementary,
Lithonia, Georgia • November/December 2008

Meeting an Author at a Convention?

If you are attending a convention and hope to meet an author, make sure you take a camera. Ahead of time, purchase a mat for a 4 by 6-inch photo. Have the author sign the mat and take a photo. After the convention, you can use the mat to frame the photo and create a display in the library.

Mary Croix Ludwick, Thomas Haley Elementary K-5,
Irving ISD, Texas • November/December 2007

Germ Fighting

If library aides or volunteer helpers use your computer, keep some germ-killing hand wipes available during flu and cold season. Your school nurse will probably have individual packets of these. Use one to go over the keyboard, the mouse, and even the gel pads to cut down on contagion. Use one on the phone as well.

Sheryl Kindle Fullner, Nooksack Valley Middle School,
Everson, Washington • October 2007

ARRANGEMENT

Graphics and Manga

To make graphics and manga easier for students to find, pull them out and put them in a separate section. Place the nonfiction graphic books near the nonfiction section and manga near the fiction. For graphic books and mangas that are fiction, use the following spine label:

GRA

FIC

[Cutter]

For nonfiction graphic books, use the following:

GRA

Dewey number

[Cutter]

This way they are easy for students to locate, especially reluctant readers and English language learner (ELL) students.

Patricia A. Porter, Gonzales (Texas) High School, August/September 2007

Guys and Gals

Display contrasting titles side by side—for instance, grouping titles under Chick Picks and Guy Faves is a hip and fun way to encourage selection. Put pictures or props of "girly" or "macho" items in your display, such as flowers, costume jewelry, and shopping bags for the ladies and toy trucks, playing cards, and sports equipment for the gentlemen. Students enjoy seeing what their peers are reading, and teachers appreciate the suggestions when directing students to find a book for an assignment.

Sharon L. Bush, West Genesee High School,
Camillus, New York • March 2006

By the Colors

Colored transparent spine labels are a great way to distinguish special categories in your library. I use green to cover the spine labels of the reference collection and red for the professional books for the staff. This is especially helpful if you have student aides assisting you in circulation and reshelving duties. The colored transparent spine labels are available from most library supply vendors.

Marilyn Eanes, Hopewell Middle School,
Round Rock, Texas • March 2007

Series Series

Our students are very interested in reading books, especially novels, that are part of a series. Although we have the series information in the library catalog, it is difficult for the "browsers" to locate this information on the shelves. To help those students, we put labels with the name of the series and the volume, if available, across the top of the spines of the books. That way, as students are browsing, they can easily see what books are in a series and in which order they should be read.

Karen Burch, William Chrisman High School,
Independence, Missouri • October 2007

FURNITURE

Slip Sliding Away

Use furniture slides to move bookshelves without having to take the books off of them first. Slides are available at the hardware store in a variety of sizes and allow you to move heavy furniture easily and without having to rely on your maintenance crew to help you out!

Catherine Trinkle, Hickory Elementary, Avon, Indiana • April/May 2008

Use Every Inch of Space—Even the Windowsills!

Our library is housed in a building with incredibly deep windowsills. We realized that these windowsills, measuring 70 inches by 27 inches, would be a great way to solve our seating shortage if we could make them into window seats. Our maintenance department verified that the windows were permanently fastened and that the structure was sound to accept weight. At a craft store, I found heavy-duty cushion foam and cut it to length for only $20 per cushion! With some inexpensive throw pillows in different sizes and sale fabric, window seats that could comfortably house two teenagers cost only $40 per window seat. This was definitely less expensive than getting two library chairs, and the kids adore the "nook" aspect of the seats. You can even just pin the fabric around the cushion so that it is easy to remove and throw in the wash.

Courtney Lewis, Kirby Library, Wyoming Seminary Upper School, Kingston, Pennsylvania • March 2007

SIGNAGE, DISPLAYS, AND BULLETIN BOARDS

Special on Aisle Four

Improving signage in the library helps students find materials. Number the aisles like a grocery store. The signs can include the call numbers of the books on each row of shelves and the major subjects of books found in those aisles. Keep a key to the aisles at the circulation desk. Not only does it allow students to browse independently; it also lets you quickly direct students and teachers to the right section of the library.

Terri Lent, Patrick Henry High School, Ashland, Virginia • August/September 2008

Quick Visible Messages

Many hardware departments carry a product called glass paint. It uncaps and has a sponge applicator that makes it easy to write on library glass doors and windows. It is designed to wipe off easily with water and paper towels without leaving residue or streaks, making it great for fast, large temporary messages. Available in most school colors, it is handy for sports phrases and spirit week or simple library newsflashes such as "Clique Books Have Arrived."

Sheryl Kindle Fullner, Nooksack Valley Middle School, Everson, Washington • March 2007

Organizing Décor

To get your monthly media center decorations neatly organized without costing you a penny, gather 18 to 20 boxes with removable lids, such as empty copy-paper boxes. Set out 9 boxes, one for each month of the school year. As one box is filled, write the name of the month on the front of it, set it aside, and put an empty box in its place. Fill the boxes until all decorations have been separated by month. Create labels for each box in a word processing program using the following settings—page setup orientation: landscape; font: Times New Roman; font size: 150. Center the text on the page. Type each month's name, print the number of labels needed for each month, and tape the labels to the shorter end of the boxes.

Judi Wollenziehn, Bishop Miege High School,
Shawnee Mission, Kansas • April/May 2008

Return to Display

About two weeks before the end of each month, pull the seasonal books for the upcoming month. Put all items on reserve for a patron named "March LMC Display" when March is approaching, for example. Circulate the items as usual; however, when they are returned and scanned, they will cause an error message to appear. The message will state that the item is "reserved for March LMC Display." Your volunteers will know exactly where to put the book: back on the monthly student display.

Beverly Frett, Robert Clow Elementary,
Naperville, Illinois • January 2006

Fancy Lettering for Bulletin Boards, Signs, and More

1. Open Microsoft Word.
2. Open a new document.
3. Click on Insert on the toolbar at the top.
4. Next, click on Picture and then on Clip Art.
5. Click on Clips Online.
6. You will see a couple of search fields near the top right-hand corner. In the box next to it, type in one of the letters that you want (whatever patterns you see for that letter, you can assume will be there for every other letter).
7. Click on Go.
8. Click on the letter that you are interested in. It will open larger in a new browser window.
9. Click on Copy. If any dialogue boxes open up, I just click on Accept, Yes, and Okay (until it goes through the downloading of Active X and the permissions).
10. Once the downloading is complete, go back into your document in Word (by clicking on that file in your toolbar at the bottom of your screen) and click on Paste (or hold down the Ctrl and V buttons at the same time to paste).
11. You may resize the letter once you have it in Word.
12. Once you are happy with that one, go back to Clip Art and follow the same directions for each letter that you need.
13. Once you have chosen your style (by clicking on one letter), you may also click on the style number to see all the letters that look like that.

Have fun decorating!

Stacy Rosenthal, Upper Moreland Middle School, Hatboro, Pennsylvania, January 2007

Shredded Paper on a Budget

Instead of buying multiple bags of expensive shredded paper in various colors, use colored butcher paper or construction paper. Run it through the school's paper shredder and use as needed.

Aileen Kirkham, Decker Prairie Elementary School Library, Magnolia, Texas • January 2008

Stick 'Em Up

Use strong magnetic cup hooks or magnetic clamps to suspend garlands, lights, posters, pictures, dream catchers, and banners from metal door and window frames. This is superior to tape or other adhesives.

Sheryl Kindle Fullner, Nooksack Valley Middle School, Everson, Washington • March/April 2009

One-Week Weeder

Once a week, haul all the books off one shelf in fiction and one in nonfiction, and put them on display. Move any books that look shabby or unloved or that are missing bar codes, spine labels, and so on into the to-do pile for that week. Select one book from the displayed books to be your favorite for when students ask. Display it on a cookbook rack or other fancy display stand with permanent words such as "Mrs. Fullner's Favorite." This ensures that by the end of the school year, you have personally handled every book and have not gotten into a rut as to which ones you promote.

Sheryl Kindle Fullner, Nooksack Valley Middle School, Everson, Washington • March 2007

Insights on Your Insides

To promote books on different medical conditions or accidents causing physical damage, suspend crutches, canes, and walking casts from the ceiling. The school nurse may have ones you can borrow. *Izzy, Willy-Nilly* (Simon Pulse, 2005) was a great excuse to hang up a jointed artificial leg that was very popular with students. Next year we will use the same garage sale prosthesis for Veterans Day or Team Able sports.

Sheryl Kindle Fullner, Nooksack Valley Middle School, Everson, Washington • May/June 2009

Time to Laminate

Because we have two laminating machines in the teachers' workroom that take a specific amount of time to warm up, I have provided an inexpensive kitchen timer for the teachers' workroom. This provides a reminder that the machines are ready when the timer rings. It also keeps the machines from being on for hours on end while someone waits for them to warm up to the appropriate temperature.

Janice Gumerman, Bingham Middle School, Independence, Missouri • January 2008

Bulletin Board Photo

Take a digital picture of your bulletin boards before you take them down and print it; tape the photo to the outside of the envelope where you store the letters and other decorations for the board. It will be easy to see in one glance the layout for the board the next time you need to put it up.

Tish Carpinelli, Lower Cape May Regional High School, Cape May, New Jersey • April/May 2007

Painter's Tape

Our library features an "Info Tank." This bulletin board is specially designated for posting information for students and faculty alike. The contents often change. Instead of using thumbtacks or staples that leave holes in the background, blue painter's tape is used to post announcements. When looped horizontally, the tape holds papers in place then peels off easily without tearing or marking the background of the board behind it.

Renee Anderson, Aurora (Illinois) Christian School • March 2007

Bulletin Board Themes

To decorate a bulletin board in the library, use a seasonal theme that also includes a library or reading slogan. Cut shapes out of extra book jackets to add a special touch to the bulletin board. For the winter holidays, cut triangle shapes from book jackets and create one large pine tree for the bulletin board. Cut heart shapes with a die-cut machine for February and create a pot of overflowing shamrock shapes for March. In the spring, try blossom shapes with three-dimensional leaves from construction paper placed in a large brown flowerpot.

Janice Gumerman, Bingham Middle School, Independence, Missouri • November/December 2006

Book Jacket Displays

If you don't have a lot of space to display books, use book jackets to display the different literary genres. On a bulletin board write down several genres, such as fiction, science fiction, historical fiction, and realistic fiction, and then glue book jackets next to each genre. Every few weeks, change the book jackets. It makes a really colorful bulletin board, and students will use it as a guide for locating books of their favorite genre.

Paty Perret Megerle, Ridgeview Elementary, San Antonio, Texas • November/December 2006

Laminate Letters

Before you cut paper for bulletin board displays with a die-cut machine, always laminate the sheets first. This process helps keep the letters stiffer to stand up to reuse year after year.

Janice Gumerman, Bingham Middle School, Independence, Missouri • November/December 2007

Organizing Bulletin Board Letters

We used to store bulletin board letters in a box, all sizes and colors in one jumble. Now we use plastic page protectors for each size and color and snap these into a three-ring binder. This takes very little room on the shelf and makes selection of letters easier, and putting them away is easy too! Just grab the page with the color of letters you will be using, and off you go!

Viola Lyons, Trinity College School, Port Hope, Ontario, October 2007

Appearance and Order

Rolling through Weeding

Tired of sore knees or sitting on the floor while working in the stacks to weed, read the shelves, or complete inventory? Use a garden/weeding cart with a seat that lifts up. This will allow you to store a laptop computer inside and run the scanner cord up through the handle area. You can be completely wireless and mobile during inventory time!

Terri Lent, Patrick Henry High School,
Ashland, Virginia • April/May 2008

Color Coordination

Many school libraries have neutral, monochromatic, or dated color schemes. One bright color can pump a huge amount of energy into the space. Our school color is purple, so at garage sales, I keep an eye out for vases, plastic containers, garlands, lights, banners, buckets—even purple spray paint—that might be put to library use. With many matching colored items in our cupboards, our library always looks coherent, trendy, and vibrant with very little expense.

Sheryl Kindle Fullner, Nooksack Valley Middle School,
Everson, Washington • April/May 2007

A Clean Slate

Take *everything* down from your walls and put up new posters every few years. This sends a message to your staff that your library is about change and promotes new ideas. It is also a great way to think about what new messages you want to convey through the posters you select.

Catherine Trinkle, Hickory Elementary,
Avon, Indiana • February 2008

Judging a Book by Its Cover

If you have books with "library bindings"—those sturdy, indestructible pebbly books of yore—put a crisp Mylar jacket on a few using a jazzy scrap of advertisement from a teen magazine and a modern font for the title and author. Some of them will probably start circulating. We all refurbish jackets from time to time, but you can add a jacket to a non-jacketed, valuable book with a dated binding.

Sheryl Fullner, Nooksack Valley Middle School,
Everson, Washington • January 2007

Art in the Library

Our library has ceiling tiles that aren't particularly pleasant to look at. In cooperation with our art teachers, we allow senior art students to borrow ceiling tiles and decorate them. When the tiles are ready, we place them back in the ceiling. Not only does our library slowly get an artistic makeover, but senior art students get to leave behind a lasting legacy. Almost everyone who enters the library enjoys this unusual art form. Students return every year to see their works of art! *Editor's note*: Be sure to get permission from the student to eventually destroy the art when the tile gets stained or worn.

Steven Reed, Wilmington High School,
Wilmington, Ohio • March 2006

Map Your World!

Show the imagination of your high school students. Line the computer lab or library walls with made-up maps. Encourage students to map their imaginary worlds as a library contest or fun activity. Topics might range from "high school hell" to "college application land," or they even may create maps based on their favorite books. This works great for computer labs used for testing when no factual information may appear on the walls.

Liz Fox, Newport (Oregon) High School • May/June 2009

Check Out These Lights

Rotate unusual lights to brighten up your library. Test and purchase novelty lights at thrift stores and garage sales. Solicit lights from vendors who run contests such as magazine sales on your campus. Purchase strings of holiday lights such as Halloween bats and Valentine hearts when they go on sale after the holiday. Fake aquariums, lava lamps, LED speaker lights, night-lights, and medusa multi-armed lights can also be rotated in. Change the light about once a month for variety, and your light collection can last for years. Store in clear plastic shoe boxes to keep cords untangled.

Sheryl Kindle Fullner, Nooksack Valley Middle School, Everson, Washington • November/December 2008

Poster Ideas

ALA posters of celebrities with their favorite books are really popular in my library, as are the free posters available at conferences. Simply tacking posters up with thumbtacks damages them and can look cheap, but buying frames is way too expensive! Our solution is to go to our local craft store and have the posters dry-mounted onto a thick poster board. It costs only around $8 per poster (for a 22- by 36-inch poster) and is incredibly lightweight. Most craft stores will even attach a little metal hanger for you! Keep a stash of them in the closet and rotate them to keep the look of the library fresh.

Courtney Lewis, Kirby Library, Wyoming Seminary Upper School, Kingston, Pennsylvania • November/December 2006

Take Your Jacket Off and Stay Awhile

When weeding the collection, make special books circulate longer by removing tattered dust jackets. Often the clean, bright hardcover underneath can allow the loved book to stand up to several more checkouts!

Tammy Sauls, Orangewood Christian School, Maitland, Florida • August/September 2007

Trash to Treasure

Don't throw away those zippered plastic bags in which linens come packaged. They make great containers for bulletin board items, puppets, seasonal decorations, and the like. They take up very little space and can even be stored in a file cabinet, alphabetized by subject with your other lesson materials. Not only does the plastic protect your possessions; you can also easily see what each bag contains.

Betsy Long, Doby's Mill Elementary, Camden, South Carolina • February 2008

Organizing Company Catalogs

To organize vendor catalogs, use a permanent Sharpie pen (this writes on all types of covers) to label the catalog. On the top left of the front cover, I write the name of the company. On the top middle, I write the type of catalog. On the top right, I put the date the catalog was received. File these in Princeton magazine files labeled with the following categories: A-V Equipment, Book Sale, Foreign Language, Computer, Library Publisher, Library Supplies, Multimedia (all types of formats), Prebound and Paperback, School Supplies, Textbook and Instructional, Vertical File, and Video or DVD. Within each file, arrange the catalogs in alphabetical order by company name. When a new catalog is received, throw away the old one and replace it with the new one. Writing the date received shows you whether the catalog is current and helps when weeding the out-of-date ones.

Dorothy Pope, Lawrence County High School,
Lawrenceburg, Tennessee • January 2006

Judge a Book by Its Cover?

Middle school students complain about taking a book with a cover, saying that the cover gets in the way or that they are afraid of losing it. Yet we noticed that if we had books on display with their covers on, students flocked to them. Because a lot of good books on the shelves were getting overlooked, we decided to put the covers back on all of our books but keep them when students check them out. The cover has a spine label, and the book has the bar-code label and a spine label. Next to the circulation desk in a file drawer, we file the covers alphabetically, according to the author's last name. As the books are checked out, covers are placed in the appropriate folder. When books are returned, covers are replaced before the books are shelved. This system seems to be working effectively. Students are discovering some great books they wouldn't have given a second thought to reading, *and* the covers are lasting.

Dena Early, Bellefontaine (Ohio) Middle School • October 2006

SUPPLIES

Down the Drain

Stationery stores carry fabulous graphic manila folders with wild designs. Use a discreet black metal dish drainer to hold a dozen of your most frequently used files upright and separated for easy access on your desk.

Sheryl Kindle Fullner, Nooksack Valley Middle School, Everson, Washington • August/September 2007

Super Tub of Fun

When students have creative projects for class, markers become a hot commodity. Knowing how easily art supplies can get misplaced, we bought an inexpensive clear plastic bin with a handle and dubbed it the "super tub of fun." It contains all the markers, crayons, glitter, glue, and stickers that we buy or collect throughout the year and is easily portable within the library. Our students enjoy asking for it, and everything stays together in one place.

Courtney Lewis, Kirby Library, Wyoming Seminary Upper School, Kingston, Pennsylvania • February 2007

Retaining the Original

When making numerous copies from a master, mark the original with "ORIGINAL" and the school year dates (e.g., "07–08") in yellow highlighter. The highlighter does not show up when you make new copies, but you always know that you are running low when you see this designation on a page in the folder where you keep the copies.

Janice Gumerman, Bingham Middle School, Independence, Missouri • October 2008

Library Duct Tape

When you receive a new school identification badge, cover it in book tape. This tape is clear and durable, and it protects the badge. It delays the return to the long line at Human Resources to get a replacement badge: *book tape, the duct tape of the library world.*

Kristi Y. Patton, Larkspur Middle School,
Virginia Beach, Virginia • October 2008

Wandering Scissors

Often teachers forget to take scissors to the workroom with them although they need to cut pages after laminating. Get some strong cord with wire in it and tie an old pair of scissors to the laminating machine with a long length of the cord. You won't lose scissors anymore.

Janice Gumerman, Bingham Middle School,
Independence, Missouri • February 2008

Supplies to Loan

When students need supplies in the library, we hand them a plastic box (the 48-ounce disposables that you can buy at the grocery store) with 10 markers, 10 colored pencils, one pair of scissors, and one bottle of glue. We take the student's ID in exchange for the box to ensure we get it back. We also tape the supply inventory inside the box so that the students know what should be returned. We have eight boxes. We also bought gallon glue refills to refill the glue.

Jennifer Alevy, Sara Poinier, and Judy Larson, Horizon High School,
Thornton, Colorado • November/December 2008

EQUIPMENT

End-of-Year Equipment Evaluations

At the end of the school year, just before the overhead projectors are returned, I distribute an equipment evaluation form to all staff and ask them to return it attached to their projector. I keep it very brief, including a choice of four boxes for them to check to describe how well they liked the machine and one box to check if the bulb needs replacing. I know that I don't need to look at a machine with the top rating, and I can also see which ones to examine more closely.

Tish Carpinelli, Lower Cape May Regional High School,
Cape May, New Jersey • April/May 2008

Equipment Purchases

Generate a basic list of classroom equipment/media with preferred vendors, brands, model numbers, and approximate prices. Keep this list on file for yourself and the school secretary for future ordering. This reduces the numbers of different bulbs and other accessories required for many different brands. You can select specific brands with a proven reliability factor too.

Aileen Kirkham, Decker Prairie Elementary School,
Magnolia, Texas • April/May 2008

Electrical Test

If you have a nonworking piece of equipment and are not sure whether it is broken or the problem is the electrical outlet, plug a handy night-light into the outlet to test it. This saves you from lugging around a lamp or other heavy equipment to check outlets.

Michelle Robertson, Park Elementary,
Tulsa, Oklahoma • October 2008

Equipment Reliability Factor

Use a silver or black permanent marker to write the arrival date on new equipment. This gives a timeline of durability when it breaks down and helps you to decide whether to reorder that brand of equipment again. If there's room on the equipment, write the date of any repairs too. Aesthetically it may not look pretty, but it's a practical way to maintain repair records and deter theft.

Aileen Kirkham, Decker Prairie Elementary School,
Magnolia, Texas • August/September 2008

Putting a Little WHITE on the Subject

Most TV monitors, DVD players, and VCRs have the "in" and "out" points clearly marked, but these markings are usually in the same color as the body of the device. Because I can't see the imprint that well, I brush a dab of correction fluid over the imprint. Now it is much easier to decipher the correct connection without having to move the equipment to better lighting!

Mary LaMar, Silver Lake (Kansas) Junior/Senior High School
• August/September 2008

Cutting the Cord

Do you have desktop computers that often get moved from one place to another? Make it hassle-free by always leaving power and Ethernet cords in place at both locations. Just pick up the computer and move it.

You'll save a lot of time and avoid having to crawl around on the floor to find the right cord or plug.

Mary Alice Anderson, Winona (Minnesota) Area Public Schools • August/September 2006

Organizing Cables and Cords

To keep extra cables and cords organized, put comparable cables into large zippered freezer bags. Write on the bag what type of cable the bag contains. Keep all bags in a file cabinet drawer. This will keep your cables from tangling and let you know at a glance what cables you have. After organizing all the cables you can identify, take a digital picture of the mystery cables you cannot recognize, focusing on the end connectors. Send the photo via e-mail to all your teachers. Offer a prize (a chocolate bar is always popular!) to whoever can name the cable and its purpose.

Sarah C. Chase, Carroll Senior High School, Southlake, Texas • August/September 2006

Recycle and Reward

Two large office-supply chain stores allow certain toner and ink cartridges to be returned and recycled for a $3 merchandise credit. There are limits to how many may be returned or redeemed per day. Use the money collected from recycling to buy reading incentives or to reward library volunteers.

Sheryl Fullner, Nooksack Valley Middle School, Everson, Washington • February 2008

Mice Lockdown

To protect optical mice and computer cables from being stolen, secure them by placing a plastic self-locking tie around the connecting cables and part of the hardware on the back of the CPU unit. Students may still pull cables out of the CPU, but they will not be able to remove them without being detected.

Laura Jeanette Brown, Paint Branch High School,
Hanover, Maryland • January 2006

Those Pesky Overhead Projector Bulbs!

Our school has about six or seven different models of overhead projectors, with, of course, unique bulbs for each one. Our teachers usually don't know what type of bulb belongs to their machine and often feel uncomfortable opening up their machine. So one of the librarians has to go to their classroom and inevitably brings the wrong bulb. We've solved this problem by simply attaching a piece of tape or a label on the back of the projector with the letter acronym for the bulb, so that teachers can immediately tell us which bulb to bring when they call from their classrooms. It saves us time, and they are happier, faster!

Courtney Lewis, Wyoming Seminary Upper School,
Kingston, Pennsylvania • January 2007

It's a Shoe-In!

To organize all of your remotes, buy a few plastic, hanging shoe trees and label each pocket with the corresponding TV or projector unit name and color.

Jennifer Alevy, Sara Poinier, and Judy Larson, Horizon High School,
Thornton, Colorado • January/February 2009

Oh, That One's Grumpy!

Name and color-code all of your equipment. For example, we have seven TV/DVD/VCR units; we named them after the Seven Dwarves and gave each a color and a picture of a dwarf, which we taped on the side of the unit. Paint the top of the corresponding remotes to match the unit.

Jennifer Alevy, Sara Poinier, and Judy Larson, Horizon High School, Thornton, Colorado • January/February 2009

Emergency Lighting

If your district is subject to occasional abrupt power outages without supplementary or emergency lighting during storms, solicit an LED lantern from your PTA, VFW, or other charitable group. The lanterns crank to replenish the battery, and the five to seven LED lights provide a safe level of illumination to continue manual jobs for staff or to facilitate evacuation of student groups. One lantern placed up high does much to diminish mayhem. The lanterns provide about five times the amount of light as a similar flashlight, and they illuminate a much larger radius.

Sheryl Kindle Fullner, Nooksack Valley Middle School, Everson, Washington • January/February 2009

In the Dark

For emergency checkout when the computers are down, have several clipboards prepared with boxes for student checkout information, including first and last name, student number, title of book, and bar code. Boxes are better than lines because they keep all the information contained instead of straggling down the page. Multiple boards speed up the checkouts. In case of power outages, store a windup flashlight with the boards.

Sheryl Kindle Fullner, Nooksack Valley Middle School, Everson, Washington • March/April 2009

Headphone Keepers

In order to help keep headphones and their wires in order, attach plastic self-stick hooks to the sides of the monitors. Then train the students to take off the headphones and replace them on the mounted hooks after use to keep the wires from getting tangled. Works like a dream. Headphones are easily visible at a glance, so you can account for every headphone.

Janice Gumerman, Bingham Middle School,
Independence, Missouri • March 2008

Tracking Equipment

To keep track of all of your equipment, use a whiteboard hanging by your equipment room. Create rows for each piece of equipment and columns for who checked items out, what equipment she took, and if she took any other equipment, such as Ethernet cords, extension cords, and so on. Color-code everything. We use erasable markers for the board and clean it off at the end of every day. Teachers sign up for equipment in advance on a sign-up sheet next to the whiteboard.

Jennifer Alevy, Sara Poinier, and Judy Larson, Horizon High School,
Thornton, Colorado • November/December 2008

Bag Those Remotes and Cables

Keep DVD remote controls and RCA cables together in resealable bags so that everything is traceable when these devices are checked out of the library for classroom use.

Janice Gumerman, Bingham Middle School,
Independence, Missouri • October 2007

Bar-Code Remotes

If you have DVD players for checkout, it is easier to label and bar-code the remotes than to bar-code the machines themselves.

Simply pull the remote out of a drawer and scan it. This helps to keep teachers accountable for the remotes that tend to get misplaced easily.

Janice Gumerman, Bingham Middle School,
Independence, Missouri • October 2007

Input/Output

Most VCRs have more than one input choice. When transferring from a mini-DV camcorder to a full-size VHS tape, it is necessary to select the correct input on the VCR in order to transfer the video. Even if you are able to view the pictures on your TV screen, the transfer may not be made if you have not made the correct input choice. Check your VCR instruction manual and the remote to identify the proper plugs and proper input choice.

Cheryl Youse, J. L. Lomax Elementary School,
Valdosta, Georgia • October 2007

ACQUISITIONS

Learn Before Buying

Do you want more information about a DVD or book? Check the company's Web site for the specific program you are reviewing. If the Web site is not listed in your material, search for more information using the name of the producer, distributor, or title. On these other sites you usually find a more detailed description than can be included in a review. These descriptions often include a preview of the program and teaching materials. For books you can often locate the author's home page and learn more there.

Anitra Gordon, Ann Arbor, Michigan • October 2008

High Flying Magazines

Magazine subscriptions are one of the first expendables in budget cutting. Solicit "air mile magazine" offers. Many people do not have enough points to actually get travel benefits and are willing to donate their magazine offers to the library. Although there may not be any teen or educational magazines in these offers, you can get golfing, cooking, ethnic, or fashion magazines, along with news magazines, for free.

Sheryl Kindle Fullner, Nooksack Valley Middle School, Everson, Washington • August/September 2008

Free Entertainment Videos and DVDs

Be alert to video stores that are going out of business. Some owners will donate VHS tapes and DVDs to schools as a tax write-off. Our school has a sizable entertainment video collection thanks to two local video store owners who allowed me to come and choose from their selection before their final sell-off. These are mostly movies on which I would not have spent money from my budget, but they are enjoyable leisure viewing for students and staff.

Tish Carpinelli, Lower Cape May Regional High School,
Cape May, New Jersey • February 2008

Processing Books and Materials

Checking Out Sets and Unusual Items

To circulate sets and unusual items, create laminated blank, bar-coded index cards. Take an 8 by 5-inch index card and cut it in half. On the non-lined side place a bar code on the center bottom and write "Title" with a line above the word. On the lined side put a line with "Sign Here" underneath it. Laminate these cards, punch a hole in the top middle, and hang them on a hook near the circulation desk. When someone wants to check out a set of markers or a set of class novels, write the title, cost, and—if it is a set of individual units—how many items in the group (e.g., class set of *Animal Farm*—32 books). Then have the person checking the item(s) out sign the lined side. In the computer scan the bar code and enter it as a temporary bar code with all the pertinent information. Then place the cards on another hook close to the first one. When the items come in, you will be able to quickly find the bar-coded index card, scan it in, wipe off the laminated card with a damp cloth, and reuse the card. Because you entered the information in the computer as a temporary item, you can print out overdue and fine slips.

Anna Brueher, Silver Stage High School,
Silver Springs, Nevada • January 2007

Book Hospital

During busy check-in time, you need a strategy for handling damaged books to expedite the check-in process. Before a book is scanned in, look over the book to check its condition. When damage is found, slip in a laminated bookmark at the point of damage to indicate the problem. The individual strips may say, for example, *page torn, ink, spine, stain, cover, wrinkled, pencil,* and *other.* Set the book aside in an appropriately decorated "Book Hospital" box so that check-in can proceed. For minor damage, remove the book from the student record. More serious damage warrants a fine, so don't check in the book, and wait to generate a fine letter during a less busy time. Once a week, make all repairs.

Pat Miller, Sue Creech Elementary,
Katy, Texas • January 2007

Free Books

Many libraries use permanent markers to write "Discard" or "Withdrawn" on the fronts of books being weeded. In the interest of recycling these to student shelves, don't molest the covers. Use a black Sharpie to write "FREE" on the bar code sticker instead.

Sheryl Kindle Fullner, Nooksack Valley Middle School,
Everson, Washington • March/April 2009

Bag Those Bits and Bytes

When I circulate small items that cannot be labeled or bar-coded, I put these in a resealable plastic sandwich-sized baggie. Then I attach the bar code to the outside of the baggie and scan that for checkout. This works well for items such as memory cards, wireless presentation devices, and flash drives. And best of all, it helps me keep track of these for inventory and end-of-year returns.

Janice Gumerman, Bingham Middle School,
Independence, Missouri • May/June 2009

One-Stop Sorting

Create "library action slips" (four quarter-pages fit well on 8½ by 11-inch paper) with a list of the most common clerical to-do items and copy them onto bright paper. Keep them handy at the circulation desk, and then just check the action needed, such as "new bar code," "new spine label," "glue/tape spine," or "reserve book for _____." Insert the action slip into the book until you have time to attend to the fixes.

Amy Linden, Bear River High School,
Grass Valley, California • May/June 2009

Manual Checkout

Sometimes you need to run a manual checkout because of problems with your circulation software. Instead of writing down the student's name and the book bar code, make a computer spreadsheet with one column for the student's name and one column for the book bar code. If your students have IDs with bar codes, this works easily. Most scanners still work even when not in the circulation software. When the books are returned, it is easy to find the bar code in the listing by using the Find function and scanning in the bar code for the book. If you have to do this for more than one day, you can easily start another spreadsheet so that you can keep your due dates straight.

Nancy LeCrone, Rockwall-Heath High School,
Heath, Texas • November/December 2006

SECTION 2:
WORKING WITH STUDENTS IN THE LIBRARY

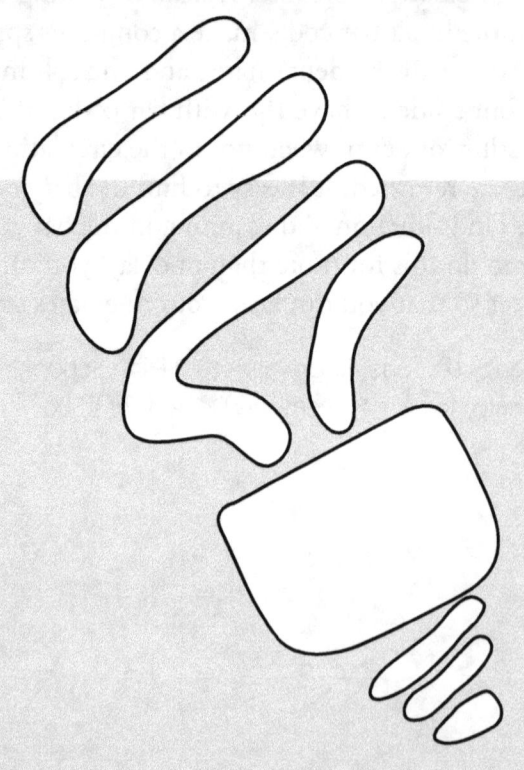

Students come to the library for many reasons. They come to do research for a specific classroom assignment or topic of interest or to check out books related to a project they are building. Some students come to the library during their study time or when they finished with a class assignment to do homework or read silently. Others may be taking tests they missed or may be seeking solace in an inclusive environment. Regardless of their reason, the secondary librarian has opportunities to establish strong positive relationships with students, staff, administrators, and community.

Tips in this section are divided into the following topics:

- Students
- Overdue Books

STUDENTS

Photographic Proof

In our litigious climate, teachers and librarians are increasingly wary of being sued. Keep an inexpensive disposable camera near your monitor. The presence of a camera is often enough to defuse a situation. Undisciplined kids may shout and berate, but solid evidence is a useful thing. The camera records events in a way that can be accepted by parents and students alike. The time required to take a photo is less than 10 seconds, so there is still plenty of time to go out into the halls and intervene for student safety if necessary.

Sheryl Kindle Fullner, Nooksack Valley Middle School, Everson, Washington • February 2007

High School Quick Reads

I keep several magazine shelves next to our magazine section for our students' favorite quick reads. Certain selections keep the section busy, such as the *Guinness Book of World Records, I Spy,* sports photo books, *The Far Side* comic books, and other special features that come and go, such as *The Osbournes, MAD* magazine special editions, sports bloopers, and various photography books. The section is great for those students sent to the library media center awaiting discipline or meetings. These books are, without a doubt, the most read books in the library media center!

Kim Clynch, Harleton (Texas) ISD Library • January 2006

Never Can Say Goodbye

Tired of raising your voice as students rush out the door, leaving the library media center in a state of chaos? Try using music as a signal five minutes before the bell rings. Choose perky goodbye songs such as "So Long, Farewell" from *The Sound of Music* or an excerpt of "Go On and Kiss Him" by the Nylons. Delegate the job of clock-watching to a student, and an orderly dismissal is in your future!

Deborah B. Ford, Instructional Media Center,
San Diego, California • January 2006

Book Holds

We love to put books on hold for students. When the book comes in, we notify their prime time (homeroom) teacher with a little note that says "Dear _____, Your student _____ has a book on hold in the Library Media Center." This has been an effective way to manage the distribution of these books at our large school. Sometimes, students come back to the library several times to see whether the book is in yet. We use that opportunity to show them some of the other items that they might find interesting.

Jennifer Dodds, South Middle School,
Grand Forks, North Dakota • January 2007

Censorship versus Selection

If some of your award-winning young adult books could be a little raw for the sixth graders in your middle school, try identifying them with movie ratings such as PG-13, sex and nudity, violence and gore, or profanity. The kids will get it, and you can talk about their family values versus censorship. A good standard line is "if this book makes you uncomfortable, bring it back right away."

Sheryl Kindle Fullner, Nooksack Valley Middle School,
Everson, Washington • January 2007

No Child Left

Sometimes librarians are responsible for teaching students how to use a mouse, a scanner, or other device that demands small motor coordination. To remind yourself how difficult this is for some beginners, use your own non-dominant hand: if you are right-handed, try it with your left.

Sheryl Fullner, Nooksack Valley Middle School,
Everson, Washington • January 2008

Promoting via Automation

Instead of listing a grade level in the library patron module, put the student's graduation year. This makes it easy to roll over records from year to year without having to edit each individual student. For example, third grade might be 2017.

Nooksack District Librarians,
Nooksack, Washington • January 2008

Post-Novel Activity

After reading a novel as a class, ask students to write down three questions they'd like to ask the book's author. Have students exchange papers and answer the questions as if they were the author. Read the questions and answers aloud for discussion.

Claudette Hegel, Bloomington,
Minnesota • January/February 2009

Topic Bingo

You can make bingo games for nearly any subject by creating cards with answers to questions. For example, entries for math can be answers to equations, and entries for vocabulary can be answers to the meaning of the words. A few other topics could be state capitals, presidents, and

Civil War facts (generals, battles, and other topics). Making the game can be time-consuming, but it can be used over and over.

Claudette Hegel, Bloomington,
Minnesota • March/April 2009

Middle School Lit Requests

Middle school students often request books of a specific type, such as tearjerkers, humorous books, sports fiction, teen pregnancy fiction, child abuse fiction, fast page turners, and so forth. It is not always easy to think of a recommendation on the spur of the moment. Keep a three-ring binder with lists related to issues teens ask about. Each time you finish reading a book, add the title and author to one of the lists.

Mavis Schipman, Douglas Middle School,
Box Elder, South Dakota • March 2006

Reason for Visit

When students come to the library, ask them to sign in on a daily log sheet. Include boxes in columns for the students to check off the reason for the visit. That way you can remind students about why they are in the library and monitor students who seem to have no purpose in the library. It also serves as written documentation for drop-in visits by students throughout the day.

Janice Gumerman, Bingham Middle School,
Independence, Missouri • November/December 2007

Book Club to Go

Our media center has a variety of novels with multiple copies. We've gathered several of the multiple titles together on one bookshelf and titled the area "Create Your Own Book Club." Groups of students are then able to check out the multiple titles, read the books at their own pace, and, if they want, use questions that we provide to guide their discussions.

Cheryl McCarthy and Dan Barrios, Adlai E. Stevenson High School, Sterling Heights, Michigan • November/December 2007

Do It Yourself

When students stop by while I have a class in session and cannot help them, I have them fill out a self-checkout slip. Students take the slip, put their name and their teacher's name on it, and place the slip in the book, which they then leave on my counter. When I am finished with my class, I check the books out to those students on the slips and deliver the books before the end of the day. The students get to check out the books they want at any time, and I don't have to worry about interruptions.

Leslie Williams, California (Missouri) Elementary • November/December 2007

Public Library Patron Number

At the beginning of the school year, ask students to write their public library patron numbers in their school planner or notebook. That way, students can access their public account while at school with your advice to place holds, do searches, and reach databases.

Sheryl Kindle Fullner, Nooksack Valley Middle School, Everson, Washington • October 2007

OVERDUE BOOKS

When They Forget Their Library Books

When students forget to return their books, I let them go ahead and select books that I save for them. We have a shelf behind the circulation desk where these titles are put aside for three days. The kids use their time in the same way as their classmates who have remembered to return their materials. It also gives the children an incentive to bring their books to the library before the next class.

Gayle Stein, Central Avenue School,
Madison, New Jersey • August/September 2008

That Was Easy!

We encourage our middle school students to renew their books when they are due, if the item is still needed. We also encourage them to renew before a fine occurs on the item. At the start of the school year, I put an Easy Button at the front desk. (You may recognize this item from the Staples office-supply commercials and can purchase one there.) The students ask why it is there, and I answer, "When you renew a book, *and* there is *not* a late fine, you may push the easy button." They respond with, "That was easy." They are thrilled. The button makes a slight noise but is good for smiles, and the positive reinforcement has paid off. Now the students ask to push the easy button when they renew. We're ahead of last year on renewals, and we've had a lot of smiles!

Tricia Baackes, Steffen Middle School,
Mequon, Wisconsin • April/May 2008

Flies and Honey

Another good way to get older students to return their library books at the end of the year is to write them a letter. A friendly letter to juniors and seniors before the school year ends gently reminds them to return their library books. Try including in the letter a list of books that area colleges are requiring their incoming freshman to read and a raffle ticket to win one of these books.

Marianne Woeste, Oakwood High School,
Dayton, Ohio • January 2007

Dealing with Fines

To get materials and fines taken care of before that hectic last week, capitalize on the success of the television show *Deal or No Deal*. Students with late books can check them in and get a "deal" on their overdue fine. For students with fines, this "deal" could be a reduced fine. Next year we hope to expand using old briefcases with an amount inside, letting students pick which case/fine they want. Of course, the success of this program is directly dependent on the longevity of the television show!

Connie K. Spotts, Lakota Freshmen School, West Chester, Ohio, November/December 2006

Traveling Book Return

For secondary schools that are very spread out, take the return box to the students. High schools and middle schools often do not have scheduled library times. Every month or so, go to the far corners of the campus with a book cart right before the first bell. Announce over the intercom that you are collecting books that need to be returned. You will have better results than fine notices produce.

Sheryl Kindle Fullner, Nooksack Valley Middle School,
Everson, Washington • November/December 2007

SECTION 3:
TEACHING RESEARCH SKILLS

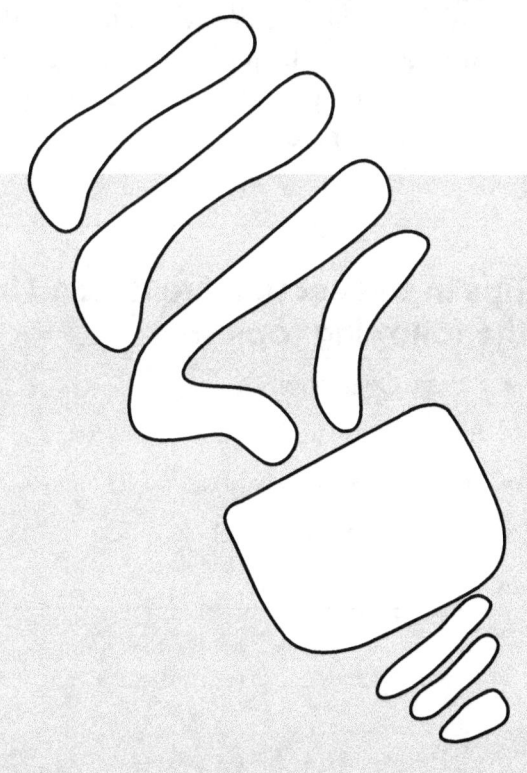

Middle and high school students learn and refine their skills in conducting research in the library and rely on the expertise of the librarian to assist them. The media specialist builds on students' previous research knowledge and helps them become more productive and information-savvy. With help from the media specialist, students learn to decipher the rich store of information that is available to them through library resources such as databases, the Internet, books, magazines, journals, and all the marvelous resources available.

Collaborating with teachers, librarians have opportunities to make the research process a positive experience, showing students how to use higher-level thinking to produce new products, strengthen original ideas, and communicate new knowledge. The media specialist of today knows that books are not relics and that the Internet is not infallible. It is his job to help students navigate and explore the available information, interpret it, and repackage it into compelling new expressions of understanding.

Tips in this section are divided into the following topics:

- Library Orientation
- Before a Research Project
- During a Research Project
- After a Research Project

LIBRARY ORIENTATION

Orientation Video

Every year, I make a new orientation video with my own narration as I walk around the media center, pointing out the important locations such as the checkout counter, book drop, and so on. This video is fun to make, and the students always enjoy watching it. It is also a great way to line up my staff and introduce them to the new students in our building. The video can be as fun as you want it to be, and it helps you rest your voice, leaving you to talk to the students about checkout procedures and other library policies once you have shown the video.

Carol Divine, Noblesville Intermediate School, Indianapolis, Indiana, August/September 2008

Pre-Searches

To keep from having to do a catalog search each time a student asks a common question, I searched all the common subjects—for example, love stories, baseball, science fiction, and relationships. I also included pertinent history subjects from which the students can choose a book for a history/social studies book report—for example, World War I, the Depression, prejudice, and Vietnam. I alphabetized all these into a notebook and put each sheet into a sheet protector. Now students can just take the sheet out of the notebook and look for books on those topics. I update the pages in the book annually to make sure the collection additions are included in the lists. I print out new lists and add them to the notebook when new common questions arise.

Frances Hazelwood, Fuqua School,
Farmville, Virginia • October 2008

Dewey Dilemma Game Using Book Jacket Covers

Collect about 20 nonfiction book jacket covers. Divide the class into teams—usually four members to a team. Give each student a copy of the Dewey decimal chart that has the numbers and descriptions of what types of books are found in each section. Each team takes a turn. Hold up a jacket cover and ask team members to confer with one another until they reach a consensus as to what section that book would fit into. I usually require that they tell me the general area rather than an exact number, but you could make it harder by asking for more specific answers. If they are right, hand them the jacket cover; if they are wrong, go to the next team until you get a correct answer. Discuss why their answer was right. The team with the most book jacket covers at the end wins prizes.

Carol Crawford, Fort Lewis Elementary, Northside Middle School,
Roanoke, Virginia • April/May 2007

Quality Questioning

To move students to higher-order thinking, try asking more "why" questions and fewer "what" questions. For example, ask, "Why do you think bears hibernate?" rather than "What do bears do during the winter?" Students are less likely to copy and paste answers from the Web if they have to provide rationale rather than simply regurgitate facts.

Donna Miller, Mesa County Valley School District 51,
Grand Junction, Colorado • August/September 2006

Quality Questioning #2: Everyone Is on the Hook!

So many times when we ask questions, the same students respond, so we really do not have an opportunity to assess whether all students in the library are engaged and learning. To prevent this situation, tell the students that when you ask a question, you want no hands raised; instead, you will select someone to answer the question. When students are uncertain about whom you will call on to answer a question, they *all* tend to pay attention.

Donna Miller, Mesa County Valley School District 51,
Grand Junction, Colorado • February 2007

Quality Questioning #3: Five "Why's"

To get students to think on a deeper level about various topics, ask "why" five times after you ask an initial question. The initial question could be one that requires a factual answer, and then you probe with five "why's" to get additional information and move students to critical thinking. Example: "What do bears do in the winter?" Answer: "They hibernate." Question: "Why do you think they hibernate?" Answer: "Because food sources are scarce in the winter." Question: "Why are food sources scarce?" Answer: "Because much of the vegetation dies." Question: "Why does vegetation die in the winter?" And so on.

Donna Miller, Mesa County Valley School District 51,
Grand Junction, Colorado • February 2007

Library Four Corners

Do your students still ask you where the fiction section is or where to find a book when the catalog tells them it's at 398.2? This game gets students better acquainted with the library than library tours do. To play, designate four places at which students can stand (the "corners") that are close to each of these sections: fiction, nonfiction, everybody, and reference. When you say "go," students quickly move to the corner of their choice. After 10 seconds, say "stop." Students still moving must go to the closest corner. Then hold up a book that is obviously from one of those corners (take these books from a box so that nobody can see what's coming next) and have students identify the area in which it would be found. Students standing in that corner sit down. Continue until only one student is left. That child gets to check out an extra book or gets to be the go/stop caller for the next game. Involve the teacher by having her show the books and act as the noise police—students who talk automatically have to sit down.

Pat Miller, Sue Creech Elementary,
Katy, Texas • March 2006

The Dewey Decimal System and Who Cares?

To help students understand the subject arrangement of nonfiction books, have some books from each classification (one classification at a time) on display by the order of the numbers, such as 100s the first time, then the 200s, and so on. In addition, put the poster for that category with the books. Change the display every two weeks. Allow students to check out these books and find replacements to continue through an entire two-week period with that number range. Hand out Dewey decimal bookmarks so that students can see what subjects will be coming up. Periodically make a school-wide announcement to highlight each of the categories and maintain interest in reading from these sections.

Sharon Thomas, Myers Middle School,
Savannah, Georgia • March 2007

BEFORE A RESEARCH PROJECT

Getting Organized for Research Papers

Our English teachers require that students turn in their note cards, copies of their sources, a rough draft, and the final research paper in a large 12 by 16-inch manila envelope. After numerous last-minute requests for envelopes, we decided to put together a research packet. We purchase the envelopes in bulk and fill them with all the essentials that students need to start their research. A sealable plastic bag is filled with a floppy disk, a highlighter, a pen, a pencil, rubber bands, paperclips, sticky notes, and note cards. A list of our remote access databases and an MLA citation sample sheet complete the package—all for $1. Surprisingly, the upperclassmen are our best customers; they know how handy this can be!

Beverly Spangler and Ann Carstarphen, Centennial High School Media Center, Roswell, Georgia • February 2007

Research Resources

To obtain good resources for literary research papers, have the teacher give you a list of all the students and the books they are researching. You will be able to pull good resources and notify the student when you find something that would be specific to her book and/or author. This could be done for any assignment when students are researching specific topics, and it is a good way to make them realize how indispensable we are.

Julie Burwinkel, Ursuline Academy, Cincinnati, Ohio • March 2008

DURING A RESEARCH PROJECT

Library Instruction Reminder Cards

To keep track of what classes need which library instruction for research projects, keep a packet of 3 by 5-inch index cards. Identify projects as "#1," "#2," and so on, using phrases that identify what you need to cover for library instruction. In your appointment book, keep track of sequential visits to the library (#1, #2, #3, etc.). Just match the card to the number (#) in the appointment book, and you're good to go. Clip these cards on a magnet over your work area until the entire research project is completed. This ensures that each class receives appropriate instruction, without forgetting something or repeating previously given instruction.

Peggy Fleming, Churchville-Chili Senior High, Churchville, New York • January/February 2009

Organize That Research Paper!

Getting high school students to understand how to organize their information for a research project is often difficult. Using a simple file folder, ask each student to label the subject of his project on the cover. Inside, glue three envelopes to each side. On the left side, the first envelope is labeled "introduction;" the second envelope is labeled "background" or "history," for example. The final envelope is labeled "conclusion." On the other side, the three envelopes have titles that reflect the subject of the project. After the student writes retrieved information on a 3 by 5-inch index card, he inserts it into the appropriate envelope in the inside of the folder. When all the information is written on the index cards and put in the labeled envelopes, the material is already organized and easier to use for the final paper. Students understand how to take notes on index cards and organize information into a final draft, and the teacher can check the student's work at each phase of the project.

Margaret Harrell, Great Bridge High School,
Chesapeake, Virginia • November/December 2006

Those Pesky Citation Examples!

No matter how many style guides and Web sites our library staff collects, there never seems to be enough citation help for students to really pinpoint how to put a bibliography together. We also run into the problem of some teachers being real sticklers about following citation styles down to the smallest details, including font size and spacing. We asked students for sample footnotes and bibliographic entries in each citation style (MLA, Chicago, APA) and ran them by our departments to make sure each department agreed these were good examples of the styles. We did a sampling of the most-asked-for examples in the library: a book, an article in a reference work, a Web site, and an article from one of our electronic databases. We've made them into both handouts and signs, and our kids use them constantly.

Courtney Lewis, Kirby Library, Wyoming Seminary Upper School,
Kingston, Pennsylvania • November/December 2006

AFTER A RESEARCH PROJECT

Research Survey

After the junior class research assignment, students fill out a survey rating the resources they used. I list all the online databases I showed them before they began their research. I ask them to indicate if they used resources from the Web, print resources from the library media center, or resources from other libraries. This identifies what resources were most valuable and assists in making budget decisions for the next school year. I also ask them if they have any "words of wisdom" to share with students who will do the research assignment next year.

Julie Burwinkel, Ursuline Academy,
Cincinnati, Ohio • January 2006

SECTION 4:

COLLABORATING WITH TEACHERS

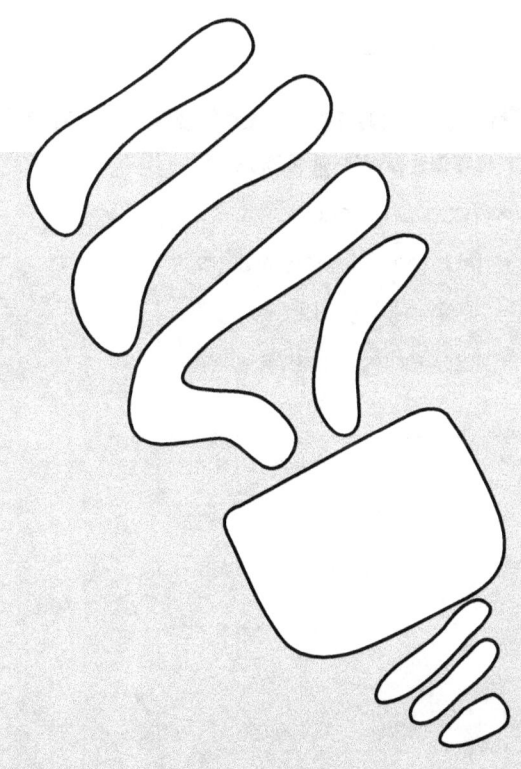

The secondary librarian has a fantastic opportunity to collaborate with his peers in all subject areas. Establishing these collaborative relationships serves many purposes and inevitably improves student learning while strengthening the media center. The librarian benefits with collection development and gains a broad view of the curriculum and instruction within the school.

By collaborating closely with the teachers in the building, the librarian can provide resources to fulfill professional needs, exchange ideas about teaching strategies and what research says is effective, and help others learn to embrace technology.

Working as a team, the librarian and her peers can exemplify for students the interconnectedness of information and provide them with a top-notch education.

The tips in this section are divided into the following topics:

- Attracting Teachers to the Library
- Promoting Library Materials
- Working Together
- Integrating Curricula

Attracting Teachers to the Library

Time Together

To make your library more inviting for teachers and staff, block off a time of "no classes" during lunchtime each day so that they can come in to eat, browse for books, and just chat with you and their colleagues. Provide coffee, tea, sweets (particularly chocolates), and other snacks to keep them coming. During book fairs, set up a special table to allow teachers and staff a place to eat in the book-laden library. Book fair sales will zoom as they come in, enjoy the new books, and put aside stacks of items they plan to purchase before the fair ends. This time together during the busy day allows all educators to maintain a good working relationship with each other.

Linda Mitchell, Indian Valley Elementary School,
Floyd County (Virginia) Public Schools • April/May 2007

The Way to Their Hearts

To show teachers your new books, throw a "Breakfast with Books" after each new shipment arrives. Offer bagels, coffee, and fruit, and display all the books you have just received. This is a great way to feed the staff and get them into the library—they love it, and the books get used!

Tara LaCerra, Westmoor Elementary School,
Northbrook, Illinois • February 2007

Teacher Feature Board

Because I review materials for *Library Media Connection*, I put a cover of the *LMC* magazine on the Teacher Feature board of the month. Each month, members of the staff put up a poster sharing information about themselves and what they do, so I included the cover from the issue with my review and the page that had my review, as well as pictures of my family. I even included a brief information document in a folder for teachers or students who wanted to know more than just the pictures showed! The students and staff enjoy learning more about each other!

Sandy Scroggs, Schenck Elementary School,
San Antonio, Texas • August/September 2007

Faculty Meeting Browsing

Many school campuses are spread out, and teachers don't get into the library media center to see what's available in the school's professional collection. To encourage teachers to browse your shelves and check out new books, set up a table prior to your faculty meeting. If your campus is wireless, checking out the books is easy with a handy laptop. Make the table really fun with posters and a tablecloth if possible. Definitely highlight books that colleagues recommend for purchase. Teachers who check out books like getting a free bookmark and chocolate too!

Andrea McDougal, Lakewood High School,
St. Petersburg, Florida • February 2008

Start the Day Right

Host an annual "Breakfast with Books" to showcase your major purchases. Show off your ordering skills when you invite the administrative team along with your staff. Make signs for picture books, fiction, professional books, poetry, nonfiction, and featured authors.

Serve pastries, fruit, and coffee, and set the atmosphere with music. Your staff will look forward to this event each spring!

Catherine Trinkle, Hickory Elementary School,
Avon, Indiana • March 2007

School-Specific Ready Reference

In order to make the library the ultimate place to go for information in the school, make a binder of all important school documents and keep it at the circulation desk. Laminate copies of "ready reference" school papers such as the hall duty schedule, a master staff and student list, fire and lockdown drill procedures, faculty meeting schedules, team assignments, homeroom numbers and teachers, the school calendar, the code of conduct, and even the teachers' contracts. Staff members know that they can quickly pop into the library to find where a teacher is on hall duty, when the next faculty meeting is, or other important everyday bits of school information!

Jacquelyn Bertalon, Woodmere Middle School,
Hewlett, New York • November/December 2008

Holiday Delights

After book orders arrive near the end of November, host a special staff day in the library called "Sweets and Treats Day." Decorate the library for the holidays. Invite staff members to have their lunch in the library on decorated tables. After their lunch, offer them a spread of homemade desserts. Display all of the new book purchases on surrounding tables and on tops of shelves. Let teachers preview and check out what's new for use in their classroom. As a parting gift, give staff members a small holiday gift from the library—usually a special bookmark, pin, or holiday antenna ball.

Diane Howes, Pecan Valley Elementary School,
San Antonio, Texas • November/December 2007

PROMOTING LIBRARY MATERIALS

Stalling New Materials

Create a word-processor document of newly arrived materials with "Come check out our new materials!" in large bold letters across the bottom. Photocopy that page onto colored paper or paper with a pretty border so that it will stand out. Post these copies in the teacher restrooms on the back of the stall doors or on the paper towel dispensers. Our teachers soon come in asking for a book or video they've seen on the list, usually within the hour.

Alicia Stratton, Jackson Road Elementary School, Griffin, Georgia • April/May 2008

Celebrate New Resources with a New Arrivals Party

Have a "new arrivals" party at the beginning of the year to show off your new resources. Decorate a section of the media center with baby shower–related items such as balloons, streamers, posters, and inexpensive table center pieces. Invite students and staff by creating baby shower invitations and placing the invitations in all the teachers' mailboxes as well as posting them around the school. Refreshments are optional but will encourage more partygoers!

Melissa Allen, Glynn Academy Media Center, Brunswick, Georgia • May/June 2009

Practice Makes Perfect

Make the faculty aware of all of the subscription databases at the beginning of the year. Then make it personal by periodically picking a different database that lends itself to a specific subject and introducing it to teachers in that subject area. Take screenshots and insert notes explaining some of the features. This works especially great for teachers of subjects such as art, foreign language, and so on who may not be aware of these resources.

Margaret Rowland, Cardinal Mooney High School,
Youngstown, Ohio • May/June 2009

Tick TOC

When you receive a new journal such as *Mailbox* or *Instructor*, make copies of the table of contents (if not prohibited by license) and put these in the teachers' mailboxes. Also put copies in the principal's box. The teachers can easily scan the contents to see if there is anything they are interested in reading. I also put copies in a notebook with dividers for each periodical—no more thumbing through issue after back issue to find that article you were looking for!

Libby McGee, Tuloso-Midway Intermediate School,
Corpus Christi, Texas • November/December 2008

Promoting Your Professional Library

Organize new professional resources with labels—such as Poetry Resources for Language Arts, Math Assessment, Utilizing Technology in the Math Classroom, or even a specific content area that the material may address. Also display professional journals with sticky notes on the cover highlighting articles of interest. As an additional resource, you can include a folder for each teacher with helpful materials such as available audio/video resources in the media center, relevant content area Web sites, and even ideas or suggestions for collaboration.

Stacy Symborski, D. R. Hill Middle School,
Lyman, South Carolina • November/December 2008

WORKING TOGETHER

Let's Get Physical!

With two New Year's resolutions to keep this year—creating more opportunities for collaboration with my teachers and taking the time to exercise at least 30 minutes every day—I decided to try combining them! To ensure my commitment to these resolutions, I sent an e-mail announcing my resolution of walking the mile that surrounds our campus during the 35-minute lunch period each day and asked if anyone wanted to come along with me.

The first day, two teachers joined me for the walk, and I found that this uninterrupted time with them allowed me to get to know them better and to talk with them about their classroom activities (and how I could help them in the library). I now get e-mails from other teachers asking me to "wait" for them on specific days during the week when they want to join me on my walk. I'm not walking with the same teachers every day, but I am making a lot of appointments with different teachers who want to join me—and when I can meet alone with one or two teachers for 20 to 30 minutes each day with an opportunity to just talk about what's happening in their classrooms, the opportunities for collaboration are certain!

Shonda Brisco, Fort Worth (Texas) Country Day School
• August/September 2006

Spread the Word

Bring professional books to your teachers. Check out professional books to "teacher's lounge," and keep them there for a couple of weeks. Then rotate them with other professional books you want your staff to be aware of. Busy teachers will appreciate the ease with which they can become familiar with this important part of the school's collection.

Catherine Trinkle, Hickory Elementary School,
Avon, Indiana • August/September 2007

Posting Lessons

Post your best lessons on your media center Web site. This allows easy access when you are sharing with colleagues or mentoring a student.

Catherine Trinkle, Hickory Elementary,
Avon, Indiana • August/September 2008

Bibliography Forms at Middle School

Although English teachers require bibliographies, other teachers sometimes ignore them for small projects because they feel bibliographies take too much class time and explanation. Make this easier for them by e-mailing all teachers proper bibliographic skeletal structure in an electronic format. Teachers can then create custom forms by selecting from the various formats: book, database, article, paper encyclopedia, electronic encyclopedia, Web site, or others that will be used in the particular project. Now all they need to do is cut and paste the number of options needed for a particular assignment. For instance, an assignment might require two books and two Web sites. The teacher creates from the template a fill-in-the-blank bibliography sheet that correlates to that assignment. Students will find it easy to staple their fill-in-the-blank bibliographies to the back of any research project.

Connie Quirk, Mickelson Middle School,
Brookings, South Dakota • August/September 2007

"Selling" Literature Circles

In an effort to promote the value of student-led book discussion groups, Literature Circles, initiate a Book Club with teachers. After school, meet on a regular basis and discuss Frank McCourt's book *Teacher Man* (Scribner, 2005). Model the discussion on the Literature Circle roles that students would be assigned in class, which include Literary Luminary, Connector, Character Captain, Artful Adventurer, and Vocabulary Enricher (see http://www.literaturecircles.com.) Teachers across all curriculums will recognize the value and success of this method and are more likely to commit to trying it with their students.

Peggy Fleming, Churchville-Chili (New York) High School
• March/April 2009

Scheduling Reminder Slip

Classroom teachers sign up to bring their classes to the media center and often forget what day and time they selected. After writing their time in the scheduling book, fill out a form for them to take, listing the date and period their classes are scheduled to visit the library media center. They appreciate the reminder, and this makes it easier for them to transfer the information into their lesson plan books.

Sample:
Your class(es) are scheduled to visit the media center on:
Date: _____
Period(s) _____

Esther Small, South High School,
Cleveland, Ohio • November/December 2008

INTEGRATING CURRICULA

Special Education Collaborations

We often overlook special education teachers in our search for collaborative partners, but in fact, our collaborations with them can be particularly fruitful. Whether you have self-contained special education classes or whether these teachers work with students for only a part of each academic day, special education teachers are often flexible and eager to try something new to benefit their students. Small research projects, author studies, and science and social studies focus work are all possible suggestions when approaching these teachers as collaborative partners.

Toni Buzzeo, Buxton, Maine • February 2007

Spreading the Word

New classroom teachers rarely learn in their graduate programs how to collaborate with the school librarian to design and/or implement research projects using library electronic and print sources. Volunteer to be a guest lecturer at local colleges with education majors. Among the topics to cover are Web site evaluation, electronic subscription databases, plagiarism, collaboration, bibliography software, and Web quests.

Peggy Fleming, Churchville-Chili Senior High School, Churchville, New York • October 2008

Poetic Science

Collaboration is a great way to reinforce the science curriculum during a poetry unit in the library. At the end, students write astronomical poetry using the poetic forms and elements taught in the poetry unit, along with the facts and information learned in science. The kids really get into this challenging culminating activity.

Nelle Coleman Cox, Dover (Delaware) Air Base
Middle School • May/June 2009

SECTION 5: USING TECHNOLOGY IN THE LIBRARY

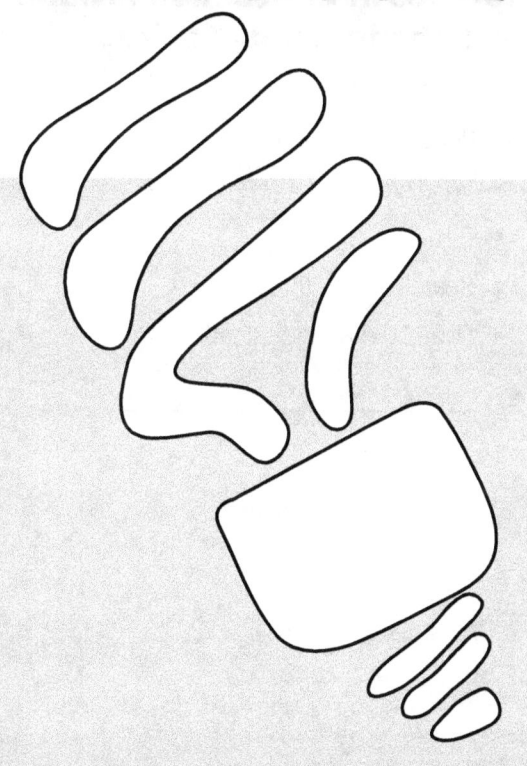

Today's students have never known life without computers. They are digital natives. They expect to find Web 2.0 tools in their school library, and they use Web 2.0 tools fearlessly and vigorously. They rely on technology to find information and to express themselves and repackage information. It is a considerable challenge for media specialists to properly facilitate students in using all of the applications, tools, search capabilities, creative software, accessories, and online communities advantageously and responsibly. Always developing, technology will continue to be one of the active and exciting roles in which the media specialist will participate.

The tips in this section include are divided into the following topics:
- Computers
- Printing
- Web Sites
- E-mail
- Searching the Internet
- Useful Library Applications

COMPUTERS

Using Technology to Teach

I collaborated with a sixth-grade language arts teacher to create short skits using a digital camera and Windows Movie Maker for the sixth-grade "Bud, Not Buddy" unit. Each student took a particular topic from the Depression era and wrote and directed the script to show his or her classmates. Students downloaded the video footage into Movie Maker and used the program as an editing tool to produce a finished movie. The students learned how to use a new program while learning about the setting of the novel.

Leslie LaMastus, Frankford Middle School Librarian,
Dallas, Texas • January 2008

Smile, Your Error Message Is on Candid Camera!

Tired of writing down error messages to report computer problems to your tech team? Using 3 by 5-inch cards, write a number for each of the computers in your media center. When an issue crops up, hold up the numbered card corresponding to the computer's number next to the screen and snap a digital picture of the error message. Attach the image to your e-mail to tech support, or print and attach it to your school work order.

Judi Wollenziehn, Bishop Miege High School,
Shawnee Mission, Kansas • January/February 2009

iSight

If you have a Macintosh computer, click on the My Computer icon to see if you have Apple Built-in iSight. If you do, look at the top of your screen and press "Take a Picture." You will immediately see what students have been looking at all day. This can be a very sobering and humbling experience, but it also opens up a quick new world for taking student pictures with their favorite books to feature as wallpaper on your library browsers.

Sheryl Kindle Fullner, Nooksack Valley Middle School,
Everson, Washington • November/December 2008

Incredible Shrinking Text

To enlarge or decrease the size of text in a word processing document or Web site, hold down the control key and then use the wheel on the mouse to either enlarge text or make it smaller.

Anitra Gordon, Ann Arbor,
Michigan • November/December 2007

PRINTING

A Printer by Any Other Name

We have had great success naming our printers from both a troubleshooting as well as a library fun standpoint. Each of our printers has a name label, so when there is a jam or need for paper refill, our students can come to us and quickly indicate which one is in trouble. I've known libraries that have named printers after famous libraries (Bodleian, Alexandria, or Library of Congress), but we have enjoyed shorter names (Lexi, Connie, Burt). It's a great idea for a contest ("Name the Library Printers!"), and students feel a great deal of ownership about the printer after it's named. When our students tell us about a paper jam, most of the time they'll say, "Lexi isn't feeling too well!"

 Courtney Lewis, Kirby Library, Wyoming Seminary Upper School, Kingston, Pennsylvania • November/December 2006

WEB SITES

Works Cited Solution

Confused about the proper way to document sources when doing research? Create a works cited page on your virtual library Web page. Include samples and instructions on how to document the resources your school provides as well as links to helpful Web sites. We followed MLA style but made some minor concessions to make the work easier for our students. Students now realize how important it is to give credit to the work of others and to follow a proper format. Because the guide is on the Web, it is always easy to use, even when students are working at home.

Carla L. Burmeister, Osseo-Fairchild Middle-High School Library, Osseo, Wisconsin • August/September 2007

Search Strategy Help for Online Databases

Always look for material that can be placed at the computers to reinforce the search skills you teach. This can be particularly useful when you are busy teaching other students or at lunch. The database providers themselves are a great place to find good free materials. Just browsing the "Help" or "Search Strategies" sections of the database will sometimes yield links to free materials you can order. EBSCOhost and Novelist supply great tri-fold search cards; these cards stand up next to computers, with three sides filled with good information and graphics, and the students find them a great refresher. They also look very impressive around the computers to parent visitors!

Courtney Lewis, Wyoming Seminary Upper School, Kingston, Pennsylvania • January 2007

Noting Great Web Sites

You probably belong to a variety of e-mail lists from which you receive e-mails filled with great ideas and suggested Web sites. Rather than stop your progress through a packed inbox to explore sites that appear interesting, keep a little notebook next to the computer. When a Web address looks tempting, jot it down in the notebook (or copy and paste it into a word processing document) and continue on with your e-mail. About once a week, set aside a little time to visit those sites and then decide which sites to bookmark or skip.

Lu Ann Staheli, Payson (Utah) Jr. High School • January 2008

Fast Drop

To access public library or government library accounts, school librarians often have to type in extremely long user numbers, 15 or more digits. To keep these handy for daily use, create a desktop file with the numbers in an easy-to-read font, separated by several lines, so that they are fast to highlight for copy-and-drop or drag-and-drop functions.

Sheryl Kindle Fullner, Nooksack Valley Middle School, Everson, Washington • March/April 2009

E-MAIL

PowerPoint PDF

To share a PowerPoint presentation on the Internet, save the presentation as a PDF document that can be viewed with Adobe Reader. The PDF presentation won't show such features as slide transitions or animations, but the information can easily be shared with anyone who has Internet access. PDFs can be viewed on Apple computers and older versions of Windows. If you use the "save as Web page" feature in Microsoft PowerPoint, only people with newer versions of Windows will be able to view the presentations.

Dawn Nakaoka, Kapalama Elementary School, Honolulu, Hawaii • August/September 2008

E-mail Binders

To prevent problems or heartache in the event that your e-mail server fails, print out messages you want to keep as soon as you read them. These may include confirmations of orders, important library or automation information, and so on. Three-hole punch the pages and arrange them in a binder, using dividers, in a manner that makes sense to you—for example, date received, subject, or topic. You can periodically check through the binder and remove messages that are no longer needed.

Laura D'Amato, Parma (Ohio) City School District • August/September 2006

Technology Resources

At the start of the school year, make technology resource bookmarks from neon-colored card stock for all of the staff. On each bookmark put the Web sites, user names, and passwords for your various electronic resources. On the back included the Web site for your OPAC and for finding Accelerated Reader quizzes.

Julie Ohrenberg, Pioneer Ridge Middle School,
Independence, Missouri • May/June 2009

SEARCHING THE INTERNET

Web Scavenger Hunts on the Go!

Need a great way to get your students to visit educational and fact-filled Web sites at recess and break time? Have a stack of pre-made Web Scavenger Hunt cards available at the circulation desk. Color-code the cards according to subject using construction paper (e.g., blue for language arts, pink for science, purple for social studies). Laminate the cards so that they will last longer. Now, when a student is caught visiting non-educational sites, you have a worthy e-alternative—and the student still gets to surf the net!

Anna Saleme, Central Catholic High School,
Morgan City, Louisiana • February 2007

Certified Searching

To short-circuit "Google-itis," we certify the students for Web searching. In other words, students move around from station to station (books, print reference resources, databases, bookmarked Web sites) and take notes and record bibliographic data at each station. They show either the classroom teacher or the librarian their note-taking sheet with information from a resource from each station. Then, and *only* then, we certify that students may move to Internet searching using Google or any other search engine. A quick and easy way to verify certification is by giving students a hand stamp (my stamp is the popular "ALA @ your library" logo, but any stamp will do). The best way to tell it's working? When students realize they've got the information they need without ever having gone to Google.

Lin Hill, Western Albemarle High School,
Crozet, Virginia • January 2007

USEFUL LIBRARY APPLICATIONS

Transferring Renaissance Records

Student records in any renaissance program can be easily exported and imported from and to any campus. Simply select the student(s) by name under the school icon within the renaissance program you are using. At the top of the screen, select the student drop-down menu, select "export," and follow the prompts. Following the same steps, files can be imported. When students transfer from one school to another in district or across the country, their renaissance records can go with them electronically. Simply attach the file and e-mail it to the person responsible for renaissance programs on the new campus. Use your librarian skills to find contact information for the old school from which a student transferred to request records.

Kaylia Thomas, Marble Falls (Texas) Independent School District • April/May 2007

Freetranslation.com

If you occasionally have to type a foreign word with special punctuation such as Español with the tilde over the "n" or Frère with an accent grave, it can be exasperating to find the right program within word processing. Put http://freetranslation.com on your favorites list. Choose the language you want, and all the punctuation (attached to the letter) is at your fingertips. Copy the letter into your document, and it will match your font and size.

Sheryl Kindle Fullner, Nooksack Valley Middle School, Everson, Washington • August/September 2007

Collection Development—Students Have Their Say

An easy way to get students' input on collection development is to create a list using a tool such as Follett Titlewave and set up a search limiting the parameters to your own specifications. For example, if you want to update your biographies, select only the interest levels "Young Adults" and "Adults for Young Adults," with the classification "Biography." Further limit your results to titles that have been reviewed by the New York Public Library Books for the Teen Age (or any other review resources you select). You can even specify a range of page numbers. Print the results in annotated format and collaborate with classroom teachers to circulate a fresh list in each of the appropriate classes for the students' input. After tabulating the results from all the classes, consider ordering the titles the students chose most often. Report back to the classes what you are ordering. The result is an updated biography (or whatever topic you chose) section with books students actually want to read, ranging from Albert Einstein to Kurt Cobain.

Sandie Liacouras, Strath Haven High School,
Wallingford, Pennsylvania • August/September 2007

Fast Reading Level

There are many online sites that publish reading levels; however, I often run across a book not listed. I quickly type a paragraph into a Word document and hit spell check. At the end of spell check, the Flesch-Kincaid Reading level appears. This process takes less than a minute and can also be done by student or parent helpers.

Sheryl Kindle Fullner, Nooksack Valley Middle School,
Everson, Washington • January 2006

ProQuest en Español

If you need resources in Spanish, try ProQuest. To pull up only articles written in Spanish, use the advanced search tab with "la(sp*)" as the first term and your subject as the second (or Boolean) term. Choosing Español from the dropdown menu in the top right corner of the ProQuest search page only changes the interface to Spanish. For example, "Search" would be changed to "Buscar," but the articles would still be in English unless "la(sp*)" is put into the search box.

Sheryl Kindle Fullner, Nooksack Valley Middle School,
Everson, Washington • November/December 2006

SECTION 6:
PROMOTING READING

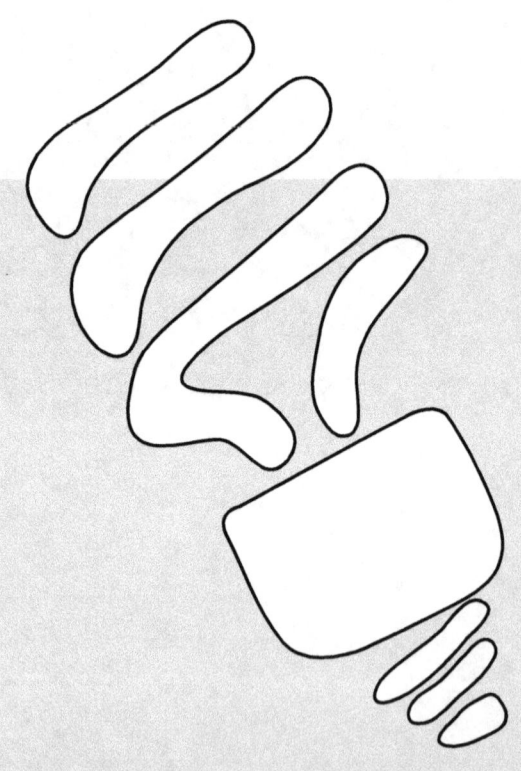

Promoting reading is a raison d'être for school librarians. Whether they are leading a book club, organizing a display for National Poetry Month, or simply talking with the students in the hallway, librarians are literacy leaders and always ambassadors for reading.

The tips in this section are divided into the following topics:

- Book Talks, Displays, and Bulletin Boards
- Reading Incentives
- Student Recommendations
- Special Events
- Special Tactics
- Utilizing Technology

BOOK TALKS, DISPLAYS, AND BULLETIN BOARDS

Brand New Books

If you are responsible for a large showcase (elementary or middle school), try a "New Edition" or "New Arrivals" display by posing your books in a doll's high chair, cradle, and carriage. If someone has a doll collection, you can also add dolls for interest.

Joan D. Villano, Fisher Middle School,
Ewing, New Jersey • February 2007

Location Is Everything

To promote the arrival of a new collection of books, open up the end of a bookshelf near the entrance to the media center. Make a few signs, and prop up a few books with old book-fair stands, and the books will be flying off the shelf! Our circulation statistics have increased *fivefold* since our first try. Location really *is* everything!

Ellen Proefrock, Lafayette-Winona Middle School,
Norfolk, Virginia • April/May 2008

Book Award Cutouts

In order to promote state award–winning books, designate a highly visible area of wall space in your media center on which to display the names of students who have read the various titles. Using a die cut resembling an open book, cut out shapes in various colors, assigning a different color for each book title. Put title and author information on a colored book shape posted on the wall, leaving room for additional shapes. When a student reads one of the titles, he writes his name on the book shape of the corresponding color. Post the shapes grouped by color with the corresponding author/title cutout on the wall.

Jane Surrency, Lake Region High School,
Eagle Lake, Florida • August/September 2008

Display Dummies

To highlight books in your collection, cover old hardcover books that are about to be weeded from your collection with brown paper bag covers. Search an online bookseller for the exact jacket of the new book(s) that you want to highlight. Print the covers on a color printer and then tape the covers to the brown paper covers. These book doubles are ready for the library display case, while the original books are available for circulation. When it is time to highlight different books, just take the color copy off the jacket and attach a new one.

Diana Wendell, Dana L. West High School,
Port Byron, New York • August/September 2008

Soupy Display

To create a quick three-dimensional display to go with your *Chicken Soup for the Soul* (Health Communications, 1993–2006) books, arrange family-size and regular-size cans of chicken soup and packages of dried chicken soup to create a hefty pyramid. Supplement this with several giant soup mugs from the thrift store. The next time your school has a food drive, you can recreate this display and see if students can collect 100 cans of soup to donate.

Sheryl Kindle Fullner, Nooksack Valley Middle School,
Everson, Washington • August/September 2006

Promoting Reading

To promote literacy throughout your school, establish a permanent "Reading" bulletin board. Ask teachers for a personal photograph taken when they were in middle school, along with the title of a book they enjoyed reading as a teen. Display these "Once upon a time . . . we read too" selections during your school's fall open house. Parents and students will enjoy seeing teachers as teen readers!

Barbara Hirsch, Hastings Middle School,
Upper Arlington, Ohio • January 2006

Other Uses for Book Jackets

So many new books now come with book jackets that have exactly the same information and illustrations printed on the front covers. Especially in junior and senior high, it is not always necessary to keep a Mylar jacket on a well-made book. Instead, process those books without their jackets, and use the jackets for bulletin boards and other displays. You can staple the jackets on a bulletin board of "New Items" or on a board with a theme you have created. Students can see the jackets on display and then check out the book(s) that caught their interest.

Trisha Lake, Elk Island Public Schools,
Sherwood Park, Alberta, Canada • January 2006

What's New in the Library Media Center?

It is difficult to get information to students on new books, sequels, or just good books to read. At our middle school, we videotape morning announcements and show them during advisory/homeroom each day. One or two times a week, we feature "What's New in the Library Media Center." Students read book reviews, list new arrivals or sequels, or feature current displays in the library media center. Students also get a glimpse of what the new books look like. Is it effective? Often the showcased book will be gone before advisory period is over!

Karen Reiber, Nagel Middle School,
Cincinnati, Ohio • January 2006

Finding a Home for a Book

We all know that book talks help get kids excited about checking out books. If your school has a daily bulletin, use that as a way to book-talk books to the entire school! Each week, select a book as the Book of the Week. Write a few catchy sentences about it, and make sure it runs each day that week in the student bulletin. Put the book on display in a prominent place on the circulation counter. If you do this properly, most of the books you highlight will be checked out by the end of the week. This is a great way to promote excellent books in your collection that don't get circulated a lot but would be read if the students knew about them.

David Bilmes, Schaghticoke Middle School,
New Milford, Connecticut • January 2007

Bookwalks

A bookwalk is a "path" created in the library using signs and book reviews written by students. Each bookwalk begins with a popular book or genre, and then students follow colored arrows to the next book. Each book is accompanied by a book summary and review. I've used this method to guide students to books they may like to read, and I include pictures of the students who wrote the reviews.

Amy Hughes, Fairmont (West Virginia) State University, January 2007

On the Fence

Our library subscribes to a monthly book service, so we receive new books all year long. When new books arrive, they go on the tables for one week, so that all classes have a chance to see what's new. Once they are available for checkout, we place them "On the Fence." The fence is one of those picket fence–style book shelves you can purchase from library supply catalogs. The students get excited after previewing the books and seeing titles they want to check out. They can't wait for the books to go "On the Fence."

Charlotte Bourdeau, Newport (North Carolina) Middle School
• March/April 2009

High-Carb Reading

My book orders suddenly filled up with bread books, and not the recipe kind: *The Breadwinner; The Bread Winner; Burned Bread and Chutney; The Risen Bread; The Bread Loaf* (poetry anthology); *Only Bread, Only Light; Peace! Land! Bread!; Peace and Bread; The White Bread Competition;* and so forth. In the past, to showcase books on the Depression era and its breadlines (such as those from the *Dear America* series), I have borrowed several automatic bread makers and purchased bread mix on sale. The wafting aroma lured some non-users of the library into my clutches. Sometimes librarians neglect the sense of smell in promoting media. Think of it as an olfactory bulletin board.

Sheryl Fullner, Nooksack Valley Middle School,
Everson, Washington • March 2006

A Poet Tree in the Library

No bulletin board has attracted as many visitors as our large paper tree filled with student-written poems. Poetry writing was the classroom activity of an English teacher who was thrilled that we highlighted her students' work. Of course, the students enjoyed sharing their efforts school-wide. The state poet laureate who had evaluated their work came to the school and awarded the local prizes in front of the library's Poet Tree.

Connie Quirk, G. S. Mickelson Middle School, Brookings, South Dakota • March 2006

Everybody Reads!

A great way to motivate students to read is to have teachers and school staff members select a book they love from your collection. Use a digital camera to take a picture of them with the book of their choice in the library. Have staff members fill out a form giving a short statement of why they love the book they have selected. Add their quotes and graphics to the pictures using appropriate software to make 11 by 14-inch or 8½ by 11-inch colored posters. Once the posters are printed on a color copier, laminate them. Display the posters with the selected books. This is a great activity that classes can work on while in the library. Each class can be responsible for a different component of the activity, or classes can do all of the components but focus on different staff members (e.g., first grade teachers, science department, building service, etc.). Students could then check out those books, or the activity could end with a school-wide event. This is a great way for a library media specialist to collaborate with teachers, focus on information literacy skills, and get everybody at the school reading.

Laura Jeanette Brown, Montgomery County Public Schools, Center for Technology Innovation, Rockville, Maryland • March 2007

Newbery Bingo

I had my students use 12 by 18-inch construction paper for the bingo boards. They cut up Follett Newbery posters into individual books and made Newbery bingo boards. The free space can be a book or the Newbery Medal from the poster. I didn't mind if each was different. I laminated them and now use them for Newbery bingo each year. It's a great way to follow up on or even introduce Newbery Medal Books. I book-talk each book as I pick it. Save a poster to cut up for your bingo call out. I make new ones each year as new books win.

Lenore Piccoli, Mount Pleasant Elementary School, Livingston, New Jersey, November/December 2007

User-Friendly, Easily Updated Reading Lists

Students like to consult recommended reading lists to find reading material, especially when the lists connect them with books they've already read. Lists such as "If You Like *Go Ask Alice*" or lists that connect readers to books that are similar to favorite television shows are very popular. But making multiple photocopies of these lists can be time-consuming and wasteful, especially when the lists are updated regularly to include new additions. Instead, I make only one, full-color copy of each of list and place each page of the list in a plastic page protector that is linked with a metal ring. Because of the page protectors, the lists can be passed around without getting destroyed as easily, and I can update the pages regularly and easily. Binding them with metal rings allows me to hang them on pegs in the library for easy access.

Cathy Belben, Burlington-Edison High School, Burlington, Washington • October 2007

READING INCENTIVES

Library Happy Meals

Homes are awash with small toys from fast-food children's meals. Collect these for unusual incentives even for high school students. One current prize at our school is a joke—plastic that looks like a spilled latte or milkshake complete with a lid and straw. Solicit these from young parents or find them at garage sales for 10 cents each or less. For younger children, purchase white paper lunch bags and combine one toy with a barely used small book. Even kindergarten student helpers can stamp designs on the bags and fold or staple them shut.

Sheryl Kindle Fullner, Nooksack Valley Middle School, Everson, Washington • October 2008

"Guess the Theme" Display

Use a special spot in the library media center to display books by theme. Change the books every week or so, on a different day each week. The first student to guess the theme of the new display wins a gel pen. This contest really gets the students looking at the displayed books and generates excitement about coming to the library media center! Themes to try include "The Eyes Have It" (*Heaven Eyes* by David Almond, *The Eyes of a Stranger* by Sharon Heisel, *The Dog with the Golden Eyes* by Frances Wilbur) and "Girlfriends" (*Goddesses: Heaven Sent* by Clea Hantman, *The Girls* by Amy Goldman Koss, *Three Girls in the City: A Self-Portrait* by Jeanne Betancourt).

Laura Stiles, Cedar Valley Middle School, Austin, Texas • January 2006

Get Tee-ed Off

Our library staff loves to wear library-messaged T-shirts and sweatshirts, but the price is prohibitive. We hosted a "design a T-shirt" contest for National Library Week. Staff and students designed original library reading messages by theme or season. We offered movie tickets and gift certificates for the winning entries, plus a library T-shirt to wear! All winning designs will be made into iron-on decals that we can put on T-shirts we already own. This contest could be used for any library promotion or seasonal theme.

Barbara Brown, Colonie Central High School Library,
Albany, New York • January 2008

Get Caught Reading!

Walk around the school and give small prizes to anyone who is actively reading a book. Prizes could be anything, including a bookmark, a pencil, or a piece of candy. Make sure students always have a book by placing a book display right at the entrance with face-front shelving. Keep the display full of new books and hot reads.

Melissa Allen, Glynn Academy,
Brunswick, Georgia • March 2008

Building a Constituency

Getting a tough, troublesome student to smile about a book is hard work for a library media specialist. When I hear a friendly "Yo, librarian lady, you gots a book on Oscar de la Hoya?" I make a note of who asked me. When the ordered book arrives, I type a large bookplate that says in bold letters, "Alejandro B. _____ advised the library media center to purchase this book." Then I take the book around and show it to the student, his friends, and his teachers. He gets dibs on the first checkout. The kids really like seeing their name in print, and the bookplate is protected with three-inch-wide library tape.

Sheryl Fullner, Nooksack Valley Middle School,
Everson, Washington • October 2006

Caught Reading

During the day in your library media center, keep an eye out for students engrossed in a book and take their picture. If you have an Ellison die cutout of a camera, place the student's picture in the center of the hole and write on the side of the cutout, "Look who was just caught reading!" Place these camera cutouts with pictures on the door of the library media center so that all can see.

Diane P. Smithson, Old Donation Center,
Virginia Beach, Virginia • October 2007

STUDENT RECOMMENDATIONS

Book Recommendation Labels

Many of us welcome student suggestions for new books. When you receive the book a student suggested, place a book donation sticker in the front with the words, "This book was suggested for our library by _____" and include the student's name and the date. Students are pleased to see themselves recognized, and they take greater ownership in their library!

Tish Carpinelli, Lower Cape May Regional High School, Cape May, New Jersey • April/May 2007

Graffiti Glass

For a library with glass doors at the entry, keep an overhead marker with dark ink near you so that students can write down book recommendations along with their names. This graffiti glass is a popular place for students to express themselves. Hand them the pen when they hand in a book. We use purple pens, our school color.

Sheryl Fullner, Nooksack Valley Middle School, Everson, Washington • January 2008

Book Display Reviews

Create a student book-review display. Take a picture of the student with the book being reviewed and place a speech balloon with his review next to the picture. Then place the book next to the photo and review.

Nelle Coleman Cox, Dover (Delaware) Air Base Middle School • May/June 2009

READ Wallpaper

Take pictures of students with their favorite new books and post them as wallpaper on the library browsers. Horizontal pictures have less distortion. Limit photos to one or two persons so that titles show up well. I put a different picture on each browser and lengthen the amount of time before the screensaver kicks in. It's great for other kids to be greeted by those book-reading smiles.

Sheryl Fullner, Nooksack Valley Middle School,
Everson, Washington • February 2008

Student Approved

I maintain a notebook of simple student reviews in the library media center. For each of the favorable reviews, I fold an index card in half lengthwise and write on the outside, "Recommended by [student's name]." I note the title and call number on the inside of the card for future use. I prop the card on the outside cover of the book on display. It is amazing to see those recommended books fly off the shelves. As an added bonus, students are eager to write more reviews so that they can see their recommended book on display. I was able to create a check-in note in our circulation program to alert me when one of the recommended books was returned, so that I can easily display it again with its card.

Marcia Krantz, Hudson Falls (New York) Middle School
• January 2006

Plate That Book

Whenever you order a book that was recommended by a student, teacher, or staff member, put a book plate designed by an art student inside the front cover, recognizing that person as the reason for purchasing the book. It could read "Suggested for your reading enjoyment by _____, Class of _____." Our students think it's great to have their names in the book.

Julie Burwinkel, Ursuline Academy,
Cincinnati, Ohio • January/February 2009

Senior Stars!

At our high school library, during May we feature "Senior Stars." Graduating seniors are invited to come to the library with a copy of one of their favorite books from elementary, middle, or high school. We take a digital picture of them posing with the book. The students write two to three sentences about why the book was memorable or meaningful to them. We make a large color poster in PowerPoint with the picture on top and the text below. We mount each poster on several colored pieces of construction paper and laminate it. The posters are featured in the library's display case during the month of May under a starry banner that reads "Starring Seniors '07!" (with the appropriate graduation year). The week before graduation, we give each student his or her poster to keep as a memento. Underclassmen, as well as teachers, love seeing what books the seniors recommend to other students to read. The seniors feel honored and valued to be featured for all the school to see.

Ellen Blumberg, Westwood High School,
Austin, Texas • March 2007

Book Recommendation Mini-Posters

Choose students who you know love to read and ask them to write down their favorite 5 to 10 books that are recent. Make a miniature poster with the student's name, a digital photo, and a list of his or her recommended books. Display it at the checkout desk. You can also make bookmarks with the same information so that the students' friends can take along their recommendations. Highlight one student at a time in a plastic sign-holder, and file the old posters in a notebook next to the current one. Students love to see what their peers are reading and enjoying!

Tish Carpinelli, Lower Cape May (New Jersey) Regional High School • October 2006

Local Celebrities

Our local Kinko's donates a monthly 24 by 36-inch full-color "READ" poster (like the ones in ALA Graphics) featuring one of our students. I take the picture and format the poster file; Kinko's does the rest! Students select a few of their favorite books from our library media center for the display case, and I type a paragraph the student writes describing why reading is important in the student's life. This case is outside the door of the library media center, which is near the front entrance of the school, so it is highly visible.

Ellen Taylor, Rossview High School, Clarksville, Tennessee • October 2006

Popsicle Stick Reviews

For a student-friendly and fun way to share student-written book reviews, have students write a five- to six-sentence review, type it up, and glue it to construction paper. Students can make it look pretty with stickers and clip art and use fancy scissors to make a unique edge to the paper. Next, laminate the reviews and glue them to a Popsicle or craft stick. The craft stick can be easily inserted into the book when the book is on display. Include a message in the circulation record indicating there is a "Popsicle stick review" available when the book is checked in, so that it can quickly go on display with the stick.

Sarah Applegate, River Ridge High School, Lacey, Washington • October 2007

SPECIAL EVENTS

Unusual Places to Advertise Programming

When my library does programming, we like to have a full-force PR campaign. Unusual flyer placement is really effective for pulling in the crowds, the secret being to place flyers where kids are a captive audience. For example, we put flyers on the library's copier lid where students have to wait while it grinds out their copies, on the door leading out of the library, in each of the computer carrels, and in the bathrooms! Although the last location may seem odd, the inside of a bathroom stall definitely appeals to a captive audience. Similarly, the mirrors that the girls and boys primp at are great to line with flyers. It is equally important to use brightly colored paper or color clip art and to keep the flyers fresh, which means having some volunteers cruise the library and school building for outdated flyers.

Courtney Lewis, Kirby Library, Wyoming Seminary Upper School, Kingston, Pennsylvania • February 2007

Make Teen Read Week Exciting

Celebrate Teen Read Week in October by hosting a Famous Monster Contest. Post pictures outside the library media center that depict a monster from a book or movie. Students give the title of the book or movie, the author of the book (if applicable), and the name of the monster portrayed in the picture gallery. Each day post a different monster's picture. We gave a $5 prize to the daily winner, and on Friday we drew a grand-prize winner from a basket of entries. The grand-prize winner won $10; our principal donated the money. Out in the hall, feature a "Horror Hall of Fame"—digital pictures of students and faculty holding their favorite horror novels. Along with the contest, the English Department read the short story "Duel," and we showed the video in the library media center during study halls.

Nancy Keenan, Glenvar High School, Roanoke (Virginia) County Schools • August/September 2006

We ♥ Reading

Our February "We Love Reading" program encourages all students to track the number of pages they read during the month of February. We track the reading by grade level using heart cutouts for each 50 pages, color-coded by grade. We also encourage each student to donate one penny for each page they read. At our school, this money is used to purchase new books for a local children's hospital. In our first year, we had 87 participants and raised $275 for new books! As students turn in their pledge forms, each one receives an "I AM LOVED" pin donated by the Helzberg Foundation (http://www.iamloved.org). We put a bookplate in the donated books that says "Donated by the Students of XYZ Elementary. We Love Reading!"

Danna DeMars, Garrett Elementary, Hazelwood, Missouri • February 2008

Book Blurbs

Avi was scheduled to come to our school. As part of our preparation, it was important for students to know he has written more than 50 books, representing a wide variety of genres. On his Web site, he has brief summaries of his books that I printed out and cut apart. I gave the students only title lists of all his works. Students worked in pairs and tried to guess which description (which I drew out of a hat and read orally) matched which title on the sheet. It kept everyone alert and actively engaged. Middle school students love competition, so I had two classes come in at a time for this activity, challenging each other with the most correct answers in the time allowed. This idea could also work with a variety of authors at a time, not just one. All you need is book blurbs for the library media specialist and a title/author list for each student or student pair.

Connie Quirk, Mickelson Middle School,
Brookings, South Dakota • January 2007

Book Fair Shopping Tips

Middle school book fairs are very successful—the students love the books *and* the extra bookmarks, pencils, erasers, and such. It can get very busy in the book fair, so to make things easier for everyone, tape one of every item on a piece of tagboard and write the price next to it. The students can easily see the price for the item they want, and the volunteers can spend their time taking money instead of talking about it! The arrangement of items stays neater too because students don't have to pick up everything to check prices before they make their purchases.

Julie Ohrenberg, Pioneer Ridge Middle School,
Independence, Missouri • January/February 2009

Candy Reading Reminders

To celebrate National Library Week, Banned Book Week, Dr. Seuss's Birthday, or other significant events for your media center, give teachers a special treat and remind them just how wonderful it is to read. Type little notes on the computer and then cut them into small strips and attach to a small piece of candy or other treat. Relate each note to reading and that specific kind of candy or treat. Following are examples of sayings:

"Be a Smartie—read a book" attached to Smarties candies

"Don't be a dud—read a book" attached to a small individual box of Milk Duds

"Knowledge gained from books can be a real 'lifesaver'" attached to a small individual roll of Lifesavers

"Books can 'rock' your world!" attached to rock candy

"Reading is 'mint' to be fun" attached to a mint

"Don't be a sucker—read a book" attached to a lollipop

"Books are number 1, and pencils are number 2" attached to a pencil

"Just wanted to keep you 'posted' that this week is National Library Week [or other event]" attached to Post-it notes

Remember to let them know whom the treat is from with a short message such as "From the Media Center. Remember to celebrate National Library Week (or other event) by reading a good book."

Melissa Allen, Glynn Academy, Brunswick, Georgia, March/April 2009

Selling AR

If Accelerated Reader motivates a lot of your students at the book fair, put a sticky note on the shelves in front of each book that has an AR quiz, indicating the book level and number of points. Many students choose books that they can use for their AR goals.

Julie Ohrenberg, Pioneer Ridge Middle School,
Independence, Missouri • March/April 2009

NLW Posters

In preparation for National Library Week, send out questionnaires via homerooms to all your middle school students. Ask the students to name their top three reasons to read and their favorite thing about the library. Their responses will be varied and often surprising. Make a list of the more creative answers and compile them into free verse poems (one or two poems per grade level depending on content ideas). Make posters of the finished poems and present them to the respective English teachers. Students are excited to see their own lines in print.

Connie Quirk, Mickelson Middle School,
Brookings, South Dakota • March 2008

SPECIAL TACTICS

Books for Underachievers

In the middle school, I placed a sign by the picture books that read "Books to Read to Younger Brothers and Sisters." That way a student wasn't embarrassed to check out an easy picture book. He or she could always say it was for the young ones at home.

Linda Walkup, Tulsa (Oklahoma) Public Schools,
Fulton Teaching and Learning Academy • August/September 2007

Book Series

For students who enjoy reading fiction books in a series, create a notebook arranged by author that you keep next to the card catalog computer at the front desk. Type the author's name at the top of the page and list books written by him or her. Then copy and paste the cover of each book from the Internet. This notebook makes a quick reference source when a student is reading a series and needs to know what book comes next. A good source for finding books in a series is http://www.fantasticfiction.com. After you print each page, use a three-hole punch and then place the page in the notebook.

Peggy Nance, Harrison (Arkansas) High School Library
• August/September 2007

Summer Book-Out

Send your library media center books on summer vacation. Students really appreciate access to your collection over the summer when they have more time to read. The Advanced Placement English students, for example, choose titles from the recommended list to prepare for the fall. Many take home the books they just couldn't find time to read during the school year. Simply set up a special due date two to three weeks into the next school year and check out the books. Advertise with a summer theme such as "Books for the Beach" or "Reading Fun in the Sun." Ask each student to sign a simple agreement and write down the number of books he or she takes home. Place a return box in the school office so that students can return the books over the summer. We started slowly by setting a limit of 10 books, but we now allow a maximum of 20 books per student. We have checked out more than 1,200 books over the past 12 years for summer reading, with very few problems.

Patricia Eloranta, Medford (Wisconsin) Area Senior High School
• January 2006

GRAB Books

We started a new collection of beginner reader and first chapter books (such as Junie B. Jones) for our ESL and special education students. We seeded the collection with donations and have called the collection GRAB books for "Get Reading a Book." We house them next to our small picture-book collection with a sign saying, "These books will help beginner readers, or you can check them out to read to your younger brothers and sisters. Enjoy!" The students who need this level of books enjoy being able to check out titles they can read, and some of our better readers get a kick out of revisiting some of their childhood favorites and check them out to read to younger siblings. We avoided calling them "easy" books, and there seems to be no stigma associated with checking out "GRAB" books.

Cindy Dobrez, Harbor Lights Middle School,
Holland, Michigan • January 2008

Series Reminders

Many books in a series are not labeled conveniently to help students know which books go next. Create custom bookmarks for popular series to assist avid readers. Each time a student says, "What come next in this series?" or "Which one is first?" hand out a bookmark to provide a quick and easy solution.

Janice Gumerman, Bingham Middle School, Independence, Missouri • January 2008

Which Book Comes Next?

Our middle school students love to read series books. They were constantly asking which book came next until we came up with this solution. We typed lists of the books in each series, such as Harry Potter, Cirque du Freak, and the Alice books; printed them on brightly colored paper; and either taped them directly to the shelves in front of a series of books or set them, in clear frames, right above a series of books. Now our students are easily able to keep track of which book they need next. I found a great list of series books at the Bettendorf Library Web page and was able to cut and paste with a minimum of time and effort. That Web address is http://www.bettendorflibrary.com/bpl-bin/series.pl.

Julie Ohrenberg, Pioneer Ridge Middle School, Independence, Missouri, January 2008

Round Robin Stories

Write a "round robin" story with the class. Discuss what the story will be about, and write it on the chalkboard or overhead projector, with each student adding a sentence. Make sure that the sentences make sense and that they move the story along. When done, rewrite the story with the students' help. Type it up and make copies for each of the students—with proper credit given to the authors, of course!

Claudette Hegel, Bloomington, Minnesota • January/February 2009

Mystery Book Contest

A monthly Mystery Book Contest promotes fiction books on the school reading list. Using a digital camera, take a picture of the front cover of a book. Then use photo or publishing software to crop the photo so that only a portion of the cover is shown. Create a contest flyer using the cropped photo. To enter the contest, students write the title of the book on an entry form. The contest generates interest in the books on the reading list, and students practice locating books in the fiction section while trying to search for the mystery book.

Dawn Nakaoka, Kapalama Elementary School, Honolulu, Hawaii • January/February 2009

Author Letters, in Brief

Instead of having students write letters to busy authors, try a postcard activity. The skill of summarizing comes in handy when little space is available.

Nelle Coleman Cox, Dover (Delaware) Air Base Middle School • March/April 2009

Get Connected!

April is National Poetry Month and the month students generally take achievement tests. Connect poetry with the achievement tests by running a poetry contest for two weeks prior to testing. The only criterion: be creative and inspirational. Students and staff submit a creative or inspirational poem about getting ready for the achievement test or about taking the achievement test. The media center can announce winners at an achievement pep rally.

Karen Reiber, Nagel Media Center, Cincinnati, Ohio • March/April 2009

Looking for Read Alikes

To create a list of books that are "read alikes," use the 690 MARC tag (local subject). When you come across a book that strongly resembles a popular or classic title, create a "Read Also" 690 record for both the original and the read alike. As an example, for books that remind you of *Hatchet,* create a subject heading titled "Read also: Hatchet." Attach that as a site subject to each book that reminds you of *Hatchet* (including *Hatchet*). When you click on the "Read also: Hatchet" heading within the record, the entire list of books that "read alike" will appear. Do that for each book that has a "read alike" in your collection.

Elizabeth Mayer, H. B. Thompson Middle School, Syosset, New York • March 2008

Remembering the Good Times

Don't you just hate it when students ask for a good book by genre and your mind goes blank? Keep a collection of hole-punched note cards listing the title, the author, and a brief annotation of the book on a ring by genre. It's easy to add cards to the file as we read new books. Use it often, and students will start using it before asking for help.

Debbie Clifford, Rachel Carson Middle School, Herndon, Virginia • May/June 2009

Commissioning Artwork from Unusual Classes

Although you may get plenty of great artwork from your art studio classes and such electives as ceramics, we find the most popular projects are from our physics classes! Physics students make mobiles (demonstrating a balanced load using found objects) and tabletop catapults (made from only paper and rubber bands), and we display them by hanging them from our acoustical ceiling and placing the catapults on the top of the library media center's low shelves. A little card indicates which student is the creator. Students bring their friends to admire their handiwork and stay to read books and magazines while we reaffirm a good relationship with our science teachers.

Courtney Lewis, Wyoming Seminary Upper School,
Kingston, Pennsylvania • October 2006

ESL Pumpkins

At our school, we have a large percentage of international students who are new to American culture. Because they are usually baffled by the celebration of Halloween, our ESL program takes a day of class and introduces them to the holiday while also teaching them how to carve a pumpkin. I always request one of the pumpkins for the library media center and display it with a card indicating the names of the students who carved it. Placing other holiday-themed books around it (horror and mystery books) makes for a great display and increases circulation. Our international students (who usually shy away from recreational print reading) are attracted to the pumpkin from their classroom experience and end up browsing and checking out some of the books. It's a great way to get this reluctant group to think of the library media center as a fun and welcoming place!

Courtney Lewis, Wyoming Seminary Upper School,
Kingston, Pennsylvania • October 2006

Puzzle of the Day

Every morning, I write a puzzle of the day on the library whiteboard. I get most of the puzzle ideas from any number of brain puzzler books. The puzzles are usually a math or word problem. Students and staff both try to solve it each day. I have a basket of pencils, pens, erasers, mini posters, plastic rings, stickers, and the like to reward the winners who solve the puzzle. I always reward the first person of the day to solve it, and often, if it is a particularly hard one to solve, the first person each class period will get a prize. It's fun and inexpensive!

Kathleen A. Nester, Downingtown (Pennsylvania) High School
West Campus • October 2007

UTILIZING TECHNOLOGY

PowerPoint Library Promotion

Four years ago, with the help of our school's technology specialist, I created a PowerPoint presentation. The slide show was set up to loop continuously. The original slides containing library rules are still alive and doing well, but the PowerPoint presentation has undergone a metamorphosis. With the use of clip art, pictures taken with a digital camera, and scanned images, a smorgasbord of colorful, eye-catching slides has emerged. Digital pictures of students caught in the act of reading, studying, doing research, or choosing a book to read fills the TV screen. Special announcements or events appear that contain important dates and times so that students can remember them. A slide honoring classes that exhibit extraordinarily good library behaviors has become quite a competition. This particular PowerPoint presentation not only has had endless possibilities but also is fun and easy to update. It is a great way to get information to the school population.

Christine Smith, Siegel Middle School, Murfreesboro, Tennessee • August/September 2006

Read Books, Save Lives

Students in grades 3 and up can improve their vocabulary while helping to end world hunger. Go to freerice.com to learn more about this computer game/program where sponsors donate 10 grains of rice to the United Nations to help feed hungry people. Scheduling a competition adds to the excitement, and the rice will just pile up.

Anitra Gordon, Ann Arbor, Michigan, January/February 2009

SECTION 7:
BUILDING POSITIVE PUBLIC RELATIONS

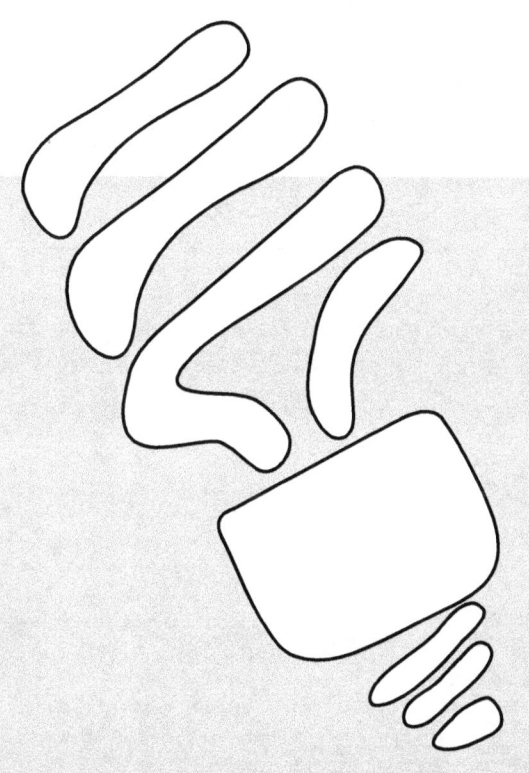

Advocacy is another premier role for the librarian. He strives daily to promote the media center and its programs to the community, parents, students, teachers, and administrators. She shows gratitude through thank-you notes and banners of acknowledgement. He seeks sponsors and collaborators by painting a vision for a dynamic and rich media center where all students learn and thrive. Positive relationships with all stakeholders help the library media specialist achieve the entire community's visions for leaning.

The tips in this section are divided into the following topics:
- Teachers and Staff
- Students
- Parents and Community
- Special Events

Teachers and Staff

Recycling for Faculty

Copier and printer paper with one side blank make great notebooks to use for taking notes at faculty meetings and workshops. Bind the paper using the spiral binding machines, and you can make any size you want, from full 8½ by 11-inch notepads to half-size or quarter-size notepads. You simply cut the spiral binder to match. You can use recycled card stock for covers. The binders can also be recycled when teachers are ready to throw away their "notebooks." This is a great task to give your student helpers. We also place quartered notepads at computer workstations. As an added touch, stamp the cover with your library information (name, address, phone number, and Web address).

Heather Loy, Wagener-Salley High School,
Wagener, South Carolina • August/September 2007

Welcome Packets

To remind administrators and teachers of the importance of the library media program, create welcome packets introducing the library resources and services and latest library study information for new staff members. Including candy or other treats will make packets stand out!

Lindsay Weaver, Walnut Creek Elementary School,
Olentangy Local Schools, Columbus, Ohio • April/May 2007

Pony Express

When a teacher e-mails a desperate plea for quick resources, deliver them. It is amazing the amount of goodwill that can be generated for your library by the simple act of putting materials on a teacher's desk instead of merely saying that they are available for pickup in the library or teacher's box. If necessary, commandeer a student as courier, but get the resources there with jaw-dropping promptness.

Sheryl Kindle Fullner, Nooksack Valley Middle School, Everson, Washington • April/May 2008

State of the Library Address

At the end of each month, create a State of the Library Address. Because our principals look to us for data on student learning, this is a great way to give relevant library data and information without overwhelming the administrator with facts and figures. This communication allows administrators to be well informed about library usage. It is also a great time to compliment teachers who have collaborated and used the library well, and it can include information about upcoming events and activities.

Lindsay Weaver, Walnut Creek Elementary School, Columbus, Ohio • March 2007

Spoiling Teachers

Any teacher or volunteer who has a minor emergency heads for the library media center. We are fortunate to have an adult bathroom in our library media center. I keep it stocked with an SOS basket that contains hair spray, lotion, breath mints, a sewing kit, a simple first aid kit, safety pins, clear nail polish, hem tape, a lint brush, and deodorant spray. We keep feminine items under the table skirt. Chocolate, tea bags, and cocoa mix are kept in the office. The goodwill generated by our dollar-store purchases is well worth the expenditure.

Pat Miller, Sue Creech Elementary, Katy ISD, Texas • January 2006

Did It Come in Yet?

Teachers need to become familiar with new books purchased with them in mind, but connecting the two can sometimes be a struggle. Make a photocopy of the cover of the new book and put it in the teacher's mailbox. The teacher can file it with the appropriate unit as a nice reminder later.

Connie Quirk, Mickelson Middle School,
Brookings, South Dakota • January 2006

Reaching Student Teachers

Looking for a way to connect with new student teachers? I invite them to the media center for a tour of the facility; I show them how to search the OPAC, highlight our district library media center Web site, and spend a few minutes showing them how to use our online databases. I also explain some of the other services our media center offers. I provide printed copies of the media center Web site homepage and information with user names and passwords for home access to the databases. I ask the student teachers right off the bat if there's anything I can do to help them, and I check in with them periodically throughout their time in the building. It's been a big success.

Laura D'Amato, Thoreau Park Elementary, Renwood Elementary,
Parma, Ohio • March 2006

Staff Photocopies for New Teachers

When making up goodie packages for new teachers each summer, always include a set of photocopies of your staff from the yearbook. With many teachers and administrators, new staff can sometimes be overwhelmed with names. This way, at least they can learn the teachers from their department, as well as have a reference for other staff. It is always a well-received welcome gift!

Tish Carpinelli, Lower Cape May Regional High School,
Cape May, New Jersey • March 2007

How about You?

Add a friendly reading nudge to your e-mail signature by including a line that reads, "I'm reading _____ _____ _____ by _____ _____. How about you?" It's fun to see what everyone is reading, and this serves as a model to everyone we communicate with, demonstrating that we practice what we preach!

Brooks Spencer, Osceola Middle School,
Ocala, Florida • May/June 2009

LMC Welcome

To new teachers or student teachers send a letter of welcome and an explanation of your LMC services. Also send a photocopy, taken from your most recent school yearbook, of your school staff—teachers, secretaries, custodians, everyone! This is a great way to meet each new addition to the staff because they invariably stop by the LMC to express thanks and to introduce themselves. I believe this icebreaker ensures they will return to us when the need arises.

Barbara Bomber, Northstar Middle School,
Eau Claire, Wisconsin • January 2007

STUDENTS

Wall of Fame

Students love to look at themselves in pictures. In order to create an environment where students feel like they are a part of the library, clip student pictures from the local newspaper. Paste the pictures on colorful construction paper and create a "Wall of Fame." Students love to enter the library and locate their pictures on the wall. Keep the pictures on the wall for the current school year and then file the pictures by year. They come in handy for parent night and open house.

Jennifer Regel Parker, Magee (Mississippi) High School • August/September 2008

Summer Bookmarks

Before the end of the school year, make summer bookmarks for each grade level to showcase some of the favorite books for the year. Include the title and author of each book with additional sections for notable authors and some popular teen-read Web sites. Book-talk a few titles you know will get their attention. During the book talk, promote the public libraries and their summer reading programs.

Leslie LaMastus, Frankford Middle School Librarian, Dallas, Texas • March 2008

Stuck on You

On 1 by 3-inch labels, print the URL of your library media center's electronic catalog. Attach these to the back side of bookmarks.

Because the students love free bookmarks, chances are that someone along the way will see the URL.

Janice Gumerman, Bingham Middle School, Independence, Missouri • October 2006

Book Fair Bookmarks

As part of your promotion for upcoming book fairs in the library, send home the usual parent letters, make verbal announcements, and put up posters with dates and times. In addition, make bookmarks out of card stock with a condensed form of the poster information. These seem to be much easier to keep track of for the students. I keep a supply in the bookmark holder on the library check-out counter and also hand them out when a student asks, "How long does the book fair last?"

Janice Gumerman, Bingham Middle School, Independence, Missouri • August/September 2008

Can I Have Your Autograph?

For a recent author visit, I created a bookmark featuring an annotated list of the author's books appropriate for my students. Three bookmarks fit on a sheet of regular-sized paper. I then asked the author to sign the master and requested permission to copy the bookmarks onto card stock to distribute to students. She agreed! I mailed the master to the home address that she graciously supplied, and after she returned the signed master, I photocopied it and passed out the signed bookmarks to the students who attended the author sessions. This way, every student had a signed item, even if they did not purchase one of the author's books!

Janice Gumerman, Bingham Middle School, Independence, Missouri • February 2008

On to LC!

Practically all of our seniors go on to college. I buy the Library of Congress classification bookmarks from the ALA store and give one to each of the seniors. It is a useful tool for them when they use their college or university library for the first time.

Julie Burwinkel, Ursuline Academy,
Cincinnati, Ohio • October 2007

PARENTS AND COMMUNITY

Partnership with the Public Library

Because students should become lifelong library users, I always get handouts from our local public library and advertise its schedule and special events in a prominent area in the school library. Also, I invite the local public library children's librarian to come and sign up our students for public library cards. This way, children who don't normally use the public library already know someone there and are more likely to visit.

Geri Ellner Krim, Far Rockaway (New York)
High School • August/September 2006

Outreach to Parents

How can librarians use parent conference days to their best advantage? Parents are very grateful to learn technology skills, at their own pace, with assistance available. Offer to teach parents to use the online databases. Include your invitation to the library with the letter sent to parents to schedule their appointments with teachers. Give parents a brief library orientation to the OPAC and to the location of books within the library. If school policy allows, issue them their own library card. Introduce them to the online databases, such as EBSCO or ProQuest, to show them how to find the latest issues of their favorite magazine. It is especially attractive to have the latest articles available online for free. Show them how to search for subjects, do a Boolean search, and use truncation. Give them time to explore the databases on their own, and then offer to answer their questions. Pass out a printed sheet with all the passwords for them to take home. Have them sign in and write comments. Save these parents' comments in your portfolio for your evaluation. Alternatively, offer to attend a meeting of the parent association and present this same lesson.

Barbara Herzog, Upper School Library, American School Foundation, Mexico City, Mexico • January 2007

Cappuccino to Go

Are you thinking of adding a cappuccino bar to your library but are not sure that it will work for you? Why not try negotiating with a local convenience store to borrow one for a few days? The slowest time for many businesses is during school hours, so finding a business that is willing to work with you may be easier than you think. Offer to move the machine, pay for the product, and split the profits. Or approach the project as a fundraiser for your library and ask the business to donate the product. Either way, you will be able to determine whether a cappuccino bar is the right addition for your library.

Brook Berg, Detroit Lakes (Minnesota) Middle School • March 2006

Wishing for Amazon

Create an Amazon.com wish list for your school, and link the wish list to your library's home page so that virtual visitors can purchase librarian-selected items for the collection. Here's how:

- Create a new wish list at http://www.Amazon.com and then click on "Make this list public."

- Next, click on "Tell people about this list." The pop-up window asks, "How do you want to share your list?" You can choose to share via e-mail, by adding a button to your library's Web page, or by adding a widget showing recently added items to your Web page. This pop-up window also contains your wish list's unique URL.

- If you opt to add a button to your Web page, another pop-up window provides various icons and corresponding HTML code that may be copied and pasted into your Web page. Visitors to your site can now click on the button you've selected and visit your wish list.

Take advantage of the options for setting the quantity desired and priority for each item and for adding comments, such as "2008 Newbery Medal winner!" Don't forget to set your library's address as the mailing address for items purchased from this wish list (an option under "Edit list information"). And finally, promote your wish list at Back to School Night, PTA and Booster meetings, and even faculty meetings so that the entire community can support your library!

Amy V. Pickett, Ridley High School Librarian, Folsom, Pennsylvania, November/December 2008

Library Advisory Board Thank-You!

Free tote bags and giveaways that come from the exhibit hall at conferences are great for re-gifting. Put all the posters, sticky notes, bags, pens, and special doodads into a big box and let members of your Library Advisory Board help themselves to the items. I had them pick a number out of a hat to determine their order so that it wasn't a free-for-all, and everyone was thrilled with coming away with freebies. It was a nice thank-you to a hardworking group!

Courtney Lewis, Wyoming Seminary Upper School,
Kingston, Pennsylvania • October 2006

Donations at Book Fair

During the book fair, my parent volunteers came up with the idea of labeling blank envelopes with the following information:

Reading Program Quiz Donations

Family Name _____

Child(ren)'s Name _____

Grade _____

Donation Amount _____

The money is kept separate from the book fair proceeds. With each book fair purchase, the cashiers ask if the family would like to make a computerized reading program donation. We've been able to order quite a few quizzes with this money. Writing thank-you notes to the families who donate is a good idea, too.

Aileen Kirkham, Decker Prairie Elementary School Library,
Magnolia, Texas • March 2008

SPECIAL EVENTS

Collect and Donate!

Because librarians should be ambassadors of goodwill and get along with everyone, why not extend this role to help others outside of school? Each month, I choose a charity and collect money from the staff that is donated to a worthy cause. After I send out a school-wide e-mail, I leave an envelope and staff roster in the office. In exchange for their donations, staff members may wear jeans on Friday. Our faculty suggests organizations that they would like to support. In the past, we have donated funds to the Lymphoma and Leukemia Society, Susan G. Komen for the Cure, the Multiple Sclerosis Society, the Alzheimer's Association, and many others. Everyone is happy to participate.

Gayle Stein, Central Avenue School,
Madison, New Jersey • October 2008

Reading Slogans

To celebrate special events such as Teen Read Week or Children's Book Week in your library, have a contest in which students create reading slogans and illustrate them on bookmarks. Choose a winning design and make T-shirts containing the slogan. Sell shirts to staff members and give T-shirts to students as prizes at an annual read-in. Decorate the media center with the most colorful bookmarks. Book club members can create giant-sized versions of some of the best bookmarks to really make the media center look festive. Kids love making the bookmarks and signs, and you can save the best ones to use year after year.

Marcia Kochel, Olson Middle School,
Bloomington, Minnesota • August/September 2007

Donating for a Fine Cause

Advertise to tell students that the week's library fines will be donated to a particular school club or event. Make contributions to sports teams attending regional championships, local food banks, or other school clubs. Students are more willing to pay their fines when they know that their fellow students are benefiting. It's an easy way to involve the media center in the school community, making it a full partner in school activities.

Mary Moyer, Delsea Regional High School,
Franklinville, New Jersey • March/April 2009

Bucks for Books!

Work with your principal, PTO, and/or community business partner to promote "Bucks for Books!" with a publicized need and specific goal. Generate a flyer with simple graphics. Show how many books the library currently owns and how many you need to be an exemplary library.

Aileen Kirkham, Decker Prairie Elementary School Library,
Magnolia, Texas • November/December 2008

SECTION 8:

WORKING WITH HELPERS

In the bustle of a middle or secondary library media center, a librarian could easily get lost if it were not for the student helpers and adult volunteers who make sense of the constant commotion. Effective student helpers and adult volunteers can tip the balance in making a good library great. These volunteers shelve books, push in chairs, check in books, organize clerical work, and run passes to classrooms. They set a positive tone for the media center and reinforce the message that the school library is an inclusive and thriving place to learn. They can provide another positive voice among students and the general population. Their stories from behind the scenes can reinforce the "wow" that keeps the public interested in your media center.

The tips in this section are divided into the following topics:

- Students
- Volunteers

STUDENTS

Recycle Those Badges

Save your badge holders from professional conferences to use for your student helpers. They are much sturdier than the plastic badges you purchase. We just hang our badges in an easily accessible place, and helpers know to grab one if they are running an errand.

Creedence Spreder, Salem High School,
Virginia Beach, Virginia • August/September 2008

Evaluating Student Library Aides

For library aides who will receive credit for their volunteerism, work with them using a point system. Give them a library skills assignment to complete, plus a journal to turn in each week. In the journal they record the tasks they have done each day, using good grammar, sentence structure, and so on. Not only do they keep track of what they do, but they also are learning a job skill, given that many employers require employees to be accountable for their time. Assign points for each task and determine grades by adding journal points to the assignment points.

Ruth Fies, Clark Middle/High School,
Hammond, Indiana • January/February 2009

Staff Badges

Library aide pins are costly, difficult to put on, and most of all *unhip*. We collected lanyards with ID pockets from various conferences and designed colorful inserts for our student workers—easy, cool, and free.

Sheryl Fullner, Nooksack Valley Middle School, Everson, Washington, March 2006

VOLUNTEERS

Thanks for the Memories

Our library classes do a lot of especially memorable activities. We take a lot of digital pictures, but it is cost prohibitive to print them all out. To commemorate the events of the year, we burn a CD slide show for students and as a thank-you to our volunteers. These CDs, which the students purchase for $1 and which volunteers receive for free, are also a great resource when pursuing grants and donations: fabulous library marketing to one's community and to grantors.

Sheryl Fullner, Nooksack Valley Middle School,
Everson, Washington • February 2007

Parent Volunteers Are a Treasure

Show your volunteers how much you "treasure" their help! Purchase a bag of Nestle Treasures chocolates. In Microsoft Publisher, use the business card template to create a cute tag reading, "We TREASURE our parent helpers at [name of your media center]." Copy the cards onto card stock. Attach the tags to the candy and place them in a plastic tub. As you greet or say good-bye to parent volunteers, hand them a piece of chocolate to sweeten the gesture and ensure they'll be back to help again soon!

Janette Fluharty, AIS East, Avon, Indiana • March/April 2009

Pamper Your Parent Helpers!

Make parent volunteers feel pampered and special when they come to help. Purchase a small plastic tote or basket and fill it with hand cream, Lifesavers, mints, chocolates, a bottle of water, and so on. Using Microsoft Publisher or Word, create an attractive thank-you sign and affix it to the side of the tote. Place the tote in a convenient spot and invite parents to help themselves to a little pampering as a sign of your appreciation!

Janette Fluharty, AIS East, Avon, Indiana • May/June 2009

ABOUT THE EDITOR

Kate Vande Brake is a newspaper journalist turned education public-relations specialist turned editorial consultant. Although her career path has resembled a pebble skipping across water, her love of reading and writing has sailed with her. Vande Brake's inspirations come from the simple pleasures of life—bright colors, slapstick humor, chocolate truffles—and she is often found teaching her three-year-old son the "important" things in life, like how to catch bugs and make jokes. She enjoys taking spontaneous trips to large warehouse stores with her husband where they can sample prepared convenience foods and try to leave without a pallet of unnecessary food. Vande Brake would be lost without her closest friends who call and e-mail her several times a week to make sure she is still smiling, and her heart belongs to her faith and her family who guide her through the obstacles of life and give her an overabundance of hope and joy to pass along to others. Vande Brake is also the editor of *TEAMS: Collaborative Units that Work.*

TIPS
OF YOUR OWN

TIPS
OF YOUR OWN

TIPS
OF YOUR OWN

TIPS
OF YOUR OWN